Answering

the
CALL

The Police Response to Family and Care-giver Violence Against People with Disabilities

L'INSTITUT
ROEHER
INSTITUTE

Answering the Call: The Police Response to Family and Care-giver Violence Against People with Disabilities

Main entry under title:

Answering the call : the police response to family and care-giver violence against people with disabilities

Includes bibliographical references.
ISBN 1-895070-35-X

1. Handicapped - Canada - Abuse of - Investigation.
2. Victims of family violence - Canada. 3. Police - Canada - Response time. 4. Handicapped - Services for - Canada. I. Roeher Institute.

HV6626.7.A56 1993   362.4'0971   C93-095050-X

The Roeher Institute
Kinsmen Building
York University
4700 Keele Street
North York, Ontario
M3J 1P3
(416) 661-9611
Fax (416) 661-5701
TDD (416) 661-2023

Institute Director: Marcia H. Rioux, PhD
Project Director: Cameron Crawford
Principal Researcher and Analyst: Cameron Crawford
Editors: Laura Code and Barbara Schon
Desktop Publishing: Dean McCallum

This project was generously funded by Public Security Canada.

THE ROEHER INSTITUTE

Canada's National Institute for the Study of Public Policy Affecting Persons with an Intellectual Impairment and other Disabilities

*T*he Roeher Institute's mandate is to provide insight into the social policy, programs, laws and other features of Canadian society that affect the capacity of people with disabilities to exercise their rights and fully participate in society.

To fulfill this mandate, The Roeher Institute is engaged in many activities: research and public policy analysis; publishing; information dissemination; and training, education and leadership development.

The Roeher Institute acts as a centre for the development and exchange of ideas, all of which are founded on a new way of looking at disability and society. It critically examines issues related to the well being and human rights of persons with an intellectual impairment and other disabilities. Based on its examination of these issues, The Institute raises awareness about the barriers that affect people's full participation and prevent them from exercising their rights. The Institute also presents policy and program alternatives.

For more information about The Roeher Institute please contact us at:

**Kinsmen Building, York University, 4700 Keele Street,
North York, Ont. M3J 1P3 (416) 661-9611,
Fax: (416) 661-5701, TDD: (416) 661-2023**

Table of Contents

Foreword

C anadian and international research shows that not only are people with disabilities as likely as others to be victimized by the violence of others; in fact, they are even more likely than others to experience it. Although violence may come from many sources, family members and care-givers are the source of much of the violence encountered by people with disabilities.

Why is this happening? What puts people with disabilities at particular risk of family and care-giver violence? What is the community doing about it? In particular, what are the police doing about it?

These are important questions. For generations people with disabilities have been shut away from the community in institutions, in congregate living situations, or in their family homes where they rely on the assistance of others. It stands to reason that if family and care-giver violence is widespread in society, the impact will be especially hard on people who are unable to escape their situation.

People with disabilities are at particular risk for other reasons. Often, they haven't been allowed much control over what happens in their lives. Other people make the decisions about who their care-givers will be. Their care-givers are often in a position to decide what will and won't happen in their lives on a daily basis. If something terrible does happen, and if the care-giver is implicated, the care-giver can often find ways to prevent this from coming to other people's attention. People with disabilities are often poor as well. They usually do not have the means to buy their way out of dangerous situations. Then again, who would believe the claim of a person with a disability, a person who does not have much money or status in the community, who insists that someone has perpetrated violence against them? Surely such things don't really happen. Surely the purported victim who makes such a claim is deluded, especially if she is confused, has a hard time remembering the details, or can't tell her story clearly to others.

Society's denial of the situation has compounded the problem. The measures that could be implemented to prevent abuse from happening are not always in place in the social service system. Where, then, is the hope that the violence will stop? The arrangements that would enable victims to come forward with their stories without fear of reprisal, misunderstanding or outright disbelief aren't universally in place. Why, then, should they come forward with their stories? There are typically no working links between community groups and the police on violence and disability issues. Who has responsibility for addressing the problem? The police receive little or no training in this area. How are they to respond? The police usually do not know about disability-related organizations and groups in their area? Who should the police turn to for assistance? And the police face the challenge of satisfying a legal system that seems immobilized at the prospect of having to deal with cases that involve alleged victims who have significant disabilities. What is the incentive for the police to press charges?

As a result, victims with disabilities fall through the cracks. The perpetrators continue to walk away. The community becomes more dangerous, especially for its most vulnerable citizens.

These problems are happening at a time when public resources for special interest groups are drying up. Police budgets for training are shrinking, and communities are increasingly plagued by gang-related and other forms of violence. The demands on the police are mounting on all sides.

This research looks at such issues. It represents another effort by The Roeher Institute to uncover not only the attitudes, but the policies, systems and procedures that shape society and that often make it difficult for people with disabilities to feel safe and participate as full citizens in Canada. It points to some serious challenges that the police must wrestle with in order to fulfill their mandate to ensure public safety for all citizens. The research offers constructive policy options that could assist the police and their partners in public safety to work more effectively together in this difficult area.

The Institute appreciates the support of Public Security Canada, which was quick to recognize the importance of these issues, provided the funding for the research and showed keen interest in the project from its outset. The generous cooperation of the chiefs of police who arranged interview contacts and recognized the importance of the research was vital to complete this project. Thanks are extended to them and to the police officers and other police personnel who candidly and generously participated in the research interviews. In addition, respondents working in the social service, health and mental health sectors also provided critically important insight. Tanya Lewis, Kristen Lindell, Michael Bach and Miriam Ticoll provided invaluable assistance with various aspects of the project.

Finally, thanks are owed most of all to the many people with disabilities who have endured the violence of the people they should be able to trust and who are beginning to come forward and confront their perpetrators. Their concerns and input to this research were a guiding stimulus. It is hoped that the research will help alleviate the violence that has scarred too many lives and that it will help shape communities that will be safer and more just.

Marcia H. Rioux, PhD
Director

Introduction

On a Sunday morning in April 1993, a young man with cerebral palsy is pushed to the ground from behind by an assailant. His face is rubbed forcibly into the ground and he is robbed of $20.[1] In January, charges of rape, indecent assault, gross indecency and sexual assault are brought against a teacher of deaf students in Ontario.[2] In August 1992, the lifeless body of a five-year-old girl who was hearing- and speech-impaired is found in a dumpster near her home in Calgary.[3] In July of the same year the police begin investigating reports of sexual assaults against two female victims. They are the latest in a string of similar incidents allegedly committed against patients at a Montreal psychiatric hospital.[4] In May a woman who uses a wheelchair because of cerebral palsy tells the police that a driver of a bus service for persons with disabilities forcibly removed her from her chair, threw her over his shoulder, carried her to his apartment and repeatedly raped her. In April a counsellor at a group home is sentenced to jail for common and sexual assault against several adults in his care.[5] In March of that same year investigators search for what they call the "despicable coward" who beat, tied, robbed and threw to the hallway floor an 81-year-old woman who is disabled.[6]

The myth that our communities do not allow people with disabilities to be victimized by violence is gradually being exploded. As people with disabilities increasingly take their place alongside others in ordinary neighbourhoods, they find themselves confronting the same problems faced by other community members. One of those problems is the possibility of being a victim of abuse. Researchers are beginning to show that people with disabilities may even be at greater risk than others of being traumatized in this way.

Myths are also exploding about the institutions, group homes and other service arrangements that have been put in place to address the needs of people with disabilities. For decades these arrangements have been seen by the general public as "safe" and as providing immunity to the regular problems of the community. They have often been regarded as a means of protecting people with "special needs" from harm. However, news reports, stories told in private and a growing body of research suggest that, in fact, people with disabilities may be at particular risk of victimization in these "safe" arrangements.

The problem — some might say epidemic — of child abuse continues to be much discussed and better understood. Once again, children with disabilities cannot be assumed to be protected from abuse by virtue of their disability. In fact, a number of studies have suggested that children with disabilities are at unusually high risk of maltreatment by family members and other care providers.[7]

Where are the police in all this? How knowledgeable are they about the violence committed by family members and other care providers against people with disabilities? What are the challenges that people with disabilities face in bringing their complaints to the police? What are the challenges the police face in their attempts to respond to those complaints? This study is a preliminary examination of these questions.

The overall aim of this study is to provide some insights into the policing process around violent victimization as it affects people with disabilities. Research for the study was conducted through interviews with police officers and others working within the policing community. Respondents from police departments in large urban areas were interviewed, as well as those from smaller urban areas and rural regions of Ontario. Eight police departments were invited to participate. One declined. People with disabilities were also interviewed, as were family members and persons involved in the disability-related service sector. Literature reviews on victimization and disability, police involvement in the area of disability and the police response to victimization in particular were conducted as well.

Statistical information on victimization and disability is scarce. Accordingly, a statistical analysis on the "vulnerability" of adults with disabilities has been prepared.[8] The analysis provides insight into several factors that have been identified as placing individuals with disabilities at risk of victimization, and examines the magnitude of risk factors that concern people with disabilities in Canada.

This study is about violence and how the policing community understands the problem as it affects victims with disabilities. During the research, an effort was made *not* to limit the definition of violence, but rather to identify the actions police officers (and others) see as encompassed by the term. A particular focus of the analysis, however, is on violence that involves the victim's family members or other care-givers as perpetrators.

The term *victimization* is used throughout the report. The term is intended to mean the use of violence by perpetrators to harm individuals with disabilities. The *victim* is defined as the person who is violently harmed by the perpetrator.[9]

Disability is defined broadly in this research as meaning any limitation that significantly affects a person's mobility, agility, sight, hearing, verbal communication or intellectual functioning. It also includes limitations arising from difficulties in the psychological, emotional or mental health domain — whether the causes are biological or socioeconomic. It is recognized that social and economic factors can play a major role in the psychological disablement process. Where relevant to the discussion, the relationship between particular disabilities and victimization is explored.

Chapter 1

General Trends and Issues

A number of general trends and issues have, or potentially could have, an impact on the relationship between the police and individuals with disabilities. This chapter provides a brief overview of the trends both in policing and in the disability community. It then explores their relevance to the relationship between the police and individuals with disabilities.

The Police

The following factors have affected the style of policing in the past decade and will likely continue to have an impact for the foreseeable future: the shift towards "community policing"; the effort to have greater representation of women and people from visible minorities on police forces; the emergence of victim sensitivity and victim assistance programs; the development of police protocols and management systems to regulate the police response to a variety of complaints; and funding issues.

a. Community or Neighbourhood Policing

Police departments are shifting their perspective of the role of the police and the relationship between law enforcement officers and other members of the community. At one time it was common for police departments to operate at arm's length from the rest of the community. The major focus of police activity was law enforcement and criminal justice — crime detection, investigations and arrests. Apart from contact with perpetrators of crime and the victims of crime, the police officer might have little other professional contact with members of the community.

The increasing complexity of society over the past 50 years, however, has necessitated changes in policing styles, particularly in urban areas. The diversity of people, complex social relations between groups, the sheer size of cities, the erosion of informal social control mechanisms, poverty and social dislocation, and the increasing range of factors that affect public safety and criminal activity seriously challenge traditional models of policing. It is more widely recognized that, rather than remaining aloof from the community, police officers actually need the support of the community to prevent crime and to deal with it once it has occurred. This recognition has led to new models of policing that seek to involve individual officers more extensively in local communities.

Involvement at the community level means that officers need more knowledge about the people who live and work in a community, and more understanding of the needs and problems unique to that locale. They need more awareness of the resources and opportunities that can be drawn on to prevent crime and to address public safety issues. This has meant a shift in policing[10] — at least in some departments — from a reactive, controlling and authoritarian approach, to a more proactive, collaborative approach based on partnerships with individual community members and groups.

The organizational structure of police agencies has also been seriously challenged. Police departments have been organized along paramilitary lines. In this structure, commands originate at the top of the organization and are put into effect by the patrol or investigating officer. This presumes that those at the top of the hierarchical command structure are knowledgeable about everything that needs to be known at the grassroots level and can frame commands that will be responsive to community needs. This has proven not to be the case.

With this system being questioned, the officer who was once at the bottom of the pecking order, and who had little power within the policing structure to exercise his or her own initiative, is being handed more responsibilities. Police officers are gaining increasing freedom and responsibility to work with members of the community in designing and implementing programs and initiatives that will address neighbourhood needs. The aim is that the community will assume ownership of these initiatives while continuing to view the police as important allies and resource persons in addressing community issues.

Along with these shifts in responsibility are important modifications to command structures. Highly centralized and hierarchical systems are gradually being restructured along de-centralized, horizontal and work-team lines. These shifts in turn call for major changes in the organizational culture of police departments — the value system and logic that drives policing. Roles and responsibilities are being redefined. For example, a patrol officer may at one time have only taken initial information about an alleged sexual abuse of a woman with a disability. This information would have been passed on to senior investigating officers who would have handled the substance of the case. Now, however, patrol officers may be involved throughout the criminal investigation. They may even be the key police agent in the process. Naturally, these changes have involved a measure of anxiety, uncertainty, self-questioning and discomfort within the policing community.

These changes may potentially help increase the patrol officers' awareness of people with disabilities in the neighbourhood who are perhaps at risk of victimization, and of general community factors that put such persons at risk. The shift has the potential to mean more contact and more effective links between the police and disability organizations as well. If these opportunities are seized, the result could be more effective crime prevention initiatives. Indeed, this research identified situations where these working links between the police and members of the disabled community are emerging. Police respondents who took part in the research spoke favourably about the benefits these linkages are having on their approach to policing. It is important to note that, although the shift towards community policing is under way in many areas of the province, the advancement of any particular department depends on many factors.

b.   *Greater Representation of Women and People from Visible Minority Groups*

During the past few years there has been much discussion about the degree to which police forces reflect the make-up of their communities. Concern has been expressed, in particular, about the need for greater representation by women and people from visible minorities. Efforts have been made in a number of police departments, as part of the community policing trend, to recruit more women and people from various ethnic backgrounds. It is generally agreed that developing a police force which reflects the community of people it serves will facilitate police responsiveness to community needs, as well as strengthen community ties. There has been little indication, however, that the concern for representation in police departments has been extended to people with disabilities. In the course of the research for this study, one police informant noted that there had been an interest in hiring a person in a wheelchair but the costs of making the police station accessible proved prohibitive. As a result, the individual was not hired.

c.   *Sensitivity and Victim Assistance*

During recent years, police attention has shifted from primarily apprehending and charging perpetrators of crime to focusing on the victims of crime. In part this shift is simply a response to political demands for the police to be more sensitive in their work. On the other hand it recognizes that the major responsibility of the police is to obtain evidence about criminal activity. The more the victim can tell the police about the incident, the better the police's chances of building a solid criminal case, laying charges and obtaining court convictions against perpetrators.

For police to obtain information from victims of violence, they must find ways of interacting with victims who have often been severely traumatized by their perpetrators. This in turn means that the police have had to become more aware of the do's and don'ts of how to develop empathic relationships with victims.

To that end, it is now common for police officers to receive basic recruit training and in-service victim sensitivity training. It is also becoming more common for departments to have internal victim assistance specialists who are skilled at supporting victims involved in police investigations. This research identified that, in a few instances, sensitivity training had focused specifically on disability issues. It also found that victim assistance specialists are in a few instances becoming aware of disability-related issues that may need to be addressed during criminal investigations.

While the interest in victim sensitivity and victim assistance is a hopeful sign in the policing community, the police and the disability community are caught on the horns of a dilemma. On the one hand, the police are custodians of public order and, as such, exercise a range of social control functions. This may require them to exercise quick judgement, adopt a "take charge" approach and be emotionally distant. On the other hand, police may be called upon to intervene in situations involving major human tragedy and suffering — situations which require them to exercise sensitivity and flexibility. These demands on the police may be perceived as disparate and contradictory. Striking a workable balance to meet the requirements of a wide range of situations can be a significant challenge for officers, superiors and police trainers.

d. The Regulatory Environment

Police officers operate within a complex regulatory environment. They are constantly updated on changes in the law. They have their own protocols or procedural guidelines on any number of matters from child sexual abuse, senior abuse, wife abuse and assault, to race relations. The attorney general may require police sensitivity to particular issues. Within any particular department, a general protocol or set of guidelines may be tailored to the specific needs of particular units such as Major Crimes or Child Abuse. There may, therefore, be layer upon layer of protocols. The protocols are constantly being modified and there may not be proper coordination among them. For example, several protocols may operate in the case of a female senior citizen who is a member of a visible minority, is deaf and has been abused by her husband.

Because of the diversity of demands in these cases and the drain they can exact on scarce police resources, matters coming to police attention may have to be put in priority according to complex rating schemes. Moreover, police departments, like all public agencies, are susceptible to political pressure. A new community demand may lead the police to take a new approach or develop a protocol towards a particular matter. In turn, the police may not be able to dedicate as much attention to yesterday's "hot issue."

This complexity can mean that individual officers

have to master a multitude of detailed rules and regulations. Efforts are being made by some departments to rationalize and simplify policies and guidelines. This regulatory maze creates a crucial challenge: how to raise the profile of disability and victimization in a way that will not bury it under the avalanche of protocols and new issues facing police departments today and in the future.

e. Funding

Like most other public agencies, police departments are under pressure to maximize the effectiveness of scarce resources. One respondent indicated that only seven minutes per shift of the average patrol officer's time is spent "off task." Indeed, modern computer systems used by some departments can put in priorities and backlog the officer's tasks in such a way that as soon as one incident has been fielded the officer is directed to proceed directly to the next. In the words of several respondents, the police are "doing the best we can" in this kind of environment.[11]

As governments continue to cut their expenditures in an effort to come to terms with deficits, it is reasonable to assume that police departments will feel the funding squeeze for some time and that the concern for efficiency will remain. Yet when asked what factors might be inhibiting the police from improving their response to victims with disabilities, several respondents pointed to the need for more training. In the same breath they commented on the lack of time and funding for professional development.

The Disability Community

The past decade has been one of change for the police, and one of important developments in the disability field. Key developments and issues include: deinstitutionalization; the emergence of a disabled consumers movement; challenges to the traditional exercise of power and control on the part of people with disabilities; the effects of poverty and social disadvantage; and the impact of legislative instruments supporting the rights and citizenship of people with disabilities.

a. Deinstitutionalization

Over the past two decades more and more people with disabilities have been moving out of institutions and into the community. At the same time, many fewer people are being admitted to institutions. To a greater extent than before, people live in their own communities with family members, in group homes, in boarding homes or by themselves. Deinstitutionalization has had an impact on many families and individuals, as well as on communities and service systems across the province.

The trend towards deinstitutionalization is to be applauded. However, for people who have not experienced community life, and for communities unaccustomed to the presence of people with disabilities, these changes may present new challenges regarding the safety and well-being of people with disabilities. The police, like other members of the community, are finding that they too must adapt to these changes. For example, whereas in the past a police officer may have relied on institutional staff to deal with a victim with a mental handicap, police now often need to be aware of other resources in the community to support the individual.

b. The Consumer Movement

Key among the developments of the past decade has been the emergence of the disabled consumer movement. The movement is made up of individuals with disabilities and the self-help organizations they have put in place and now run. The organizations address a variety of disability-related issues. The movement is in many respects "cross-disability" — a loose network of organizations and individuals representing a diversity of people, disabilities and disability issues. At the national level principal organizations in this movement are the DisAbled Women's Network, the Canadian Association of Independent Living Centres, the Consumers' Mental Health Network, the Canadian Deaf and Hard of Hearing Forum, the Canadian Association of the Deaf and People First of Canada.

The consumer movement marks an important shift in thinking, policy and practice in the disability field. The movement is based on the assumption that people with disabilities, rather than health care and other professionals, are in the best position to determine their own life goals and needs, and to make arrangements to pursue those aims and address those needs. As such, the consumer movement breaks with conventional approaches to disability. The movement seeks to free people with disabilities from domination and control by professionals and other powerful elites. Increasingly, consumers are demanding to be seen and treated as equal partners in society with all the status, respect and power that is their due. They are demanding to be taken seriously.

The impact of the disabled consumer movement is felt even by traditional service-providing organizations. People with disabilities are increasingly involved on boards of directors and in committees that report to boards. Consumers are expecting to, and being enabled to, play an active role in designing policy and programs. They are also sometimes active in the delivery of disability-related services. Consumers are expecting greater accountability on the part of services to disabled consumers. In certain situations this has led to radical changes in the delivery of services.

The emergence of the consumer movement means that paternalistic and dismissive attitudes, which have sometimes characterized the way professionals — including police — treated people with disabilities in the past, have to be rethought and discarded. There is a call for new ways of relating to this large segment of the population. New relations have to be grounded in police awareness of, and respect for, the vast differences in personality, circumstances, interests, objectives, limitations and abilities in the disabled community. People with disabilities expect to have a say in the organization and delivery of services, including services provided by the police.

c. *Power and Control*

During the past decade, many people with disabilities have come to the realization that they have lived, worked, gone to school and carried out other activities in situations where others have had power over them. This awareness has led people with disabilities to strongly criticize the social relations between themselves and social institutions. This critique focuses on education and training systems, the labour market, income support systems, social services and care providers such as family members, professionals and paraprofessionals.

It is now a widespread belief among people with disabilities in Canada that the conventional balance of power must be drastically altered. No longer is it acceptable for others to look at and treat people with disabilities as if they should merely be the passive recipients of the wisdom, good judgement and "care" of others who happen to be in positions of authority. Nor is the expectation tolerable that people with disabilities will compliantly obey those who happen to have been vested with responsibility and power.

This critical perspective on the power imbalance is finding an outlet in the policies of consumer organizations. It is also manifested in their political activities directed at public and private bodies and in their research.

This perception of power relations on the part of the disabled community may include a certain wariness of the police. After all, the police have tended to portray themselves as representatives and guardians of the status quo. It will likely take considerable effort to convince members of the disabled community that the police are attempting to be innovators and to forge creative alliances with disempowered groups, alliances that do not reproduce the traditional imbalance of power in society.

d. *Poverty and Social Disadvantage*

People with disabilities have historically been poor and have faced innumerable disadvantages in education, employment, access to income support and access to health care and other services. Poor and socially disadvantaged groups have been stigmatized by society at large.

For example, recipients of income support through welfare programs have been subjected to public scrutiny. They have also borne the brunt of mounting public distrust. The sustainability and credibility of welfare programs have been fundamentally challenged by an emerging political ethos that would diminish, if not altogether dismantle, the welfare state. Because the majority of people with disabilities are effectively locked out of the labour market and have significantly lower educational attainments than others, they have few options but to rely on programs like welfare for subsistence level incomes. As a result, many people with disabilities find themselves stereotyped and stigmatized along with other poor persons.

People with disabilities have begun to challenge the social institutions that lock them disproportionately into poverty and social disadvantage. It follows that they would be critical of public agencies (including the police) which are perceived to play a role in both reflecting and shaping the attitudes of society towards poor and disadvantaged groups.

e. Rights and Citizenship

The issues and trends discussed above revolve around fundamental concerns in the disabled community about citizenship and rights. People with disabilities are expecting more than ever before to take their place alongside other citizens as full participants in society. With input from the disabled community, a variety of legal and other instruments have been created with a view to their full participation. These instruments include the *Canadian Charter of Rights and Freedoms*, provincial human rights laws and commissions, statutory and regulatory employment equity provisions and laws and policies in support of full integration in the public school system. Parliament has established a standing committee to pursue full social and economic integration of people with disabilities. Premiers' councils, advisory groups, consultative bodies and special governmental units on disability at the provincial level have been established to pursue similar aims. Important legal cases have been initiated by people with disabilities to probe the efficacy and fairness of federal and provincial laws, policies and programs.

Through active participation in the legal, policy and governmental process, people with disabilities are working towards the full realization of their equality and citizenship rights. It is to be expected that they will continue in this direction. Accordingly, the police will likely be called upon to address the particular concerns of people with disabilities in this area. The police can at least expect people with disabilities to demand equitable access to policing services, fair treatment and the protection of the law enjoyed by other citizens.

Chapter 2

Incidents and Victims

W here people with disabilities are victimized by the violence of others, what kinds of violence are they experiencing? How big is the problem? Who are the victims? This chapter examines these questions.

It is important to point out that police departments do not, as a rule, keep statistical information on incidents involving victims with disabilities.[12] None of the police respondents who were interviewed were attached to departments where such data was kept.[13] Therefore, it is impossible to determine the specific nature of the violence and the magnitude of the problem that police departments are dealing with.

The Prevalence and Kinds of Violent Incidents

a. Prevalence

Police vary widely in their estimates of how extensively people with disabilities are being violently victimized. According to some sources, there appears to be no problem at all. According to others, as many as 25 per cent of violent incidents in which the police are called to intervene involve victims who have some form of disability. Many police respondents indicated that they had absolutely no idea about the scale or nature of the problem.

Research indicates, however, that violence against people with disabilities is indeed a significant problem. For example, the DisAbled Women's Network of Canada (DAWN) found that 40 per cent of the women with disabilities who responded to their 1988 survey on violence had been either physically assaulted or raped, or abused in some other manner (see DAWN Canada, *Beating the Odds: Violence and women with disabilities,* 1989). Griffiths (in Stimpson and Best, 1991) has estimated that 83 per cent of women who are disabled will be sexually assaulted during their lifetime. The Roeher Institute (1988) reports that the prevalence of sexual and other forms of abuse of people with a mental handicap is disproportionately high. Sullivan, Vernon and Scanlan (1987) cite research studies indicating that 54 per cent of boys and 50 per cent of girls who are deaf have been sexually abused (compared to 10 per cent of hearing boys and 25 per cent of hearing girls). Various other studies point to the high incidence of abuse affecting persons with disabilities (Kohan et al., 1987; Cash and Valentine, 1987; Ulicny et al., 1990).

b. Types of Abuse

Despite the lack of clear police information, there was a general sense among police respondents that sexual abuse, sexual assault and physical abuse account for most violent incidents affecting people with disabilities where the police are called to intervene.[14] Several police respondents suggested that people with disabilities are probably being victimized by mental cruelty and verbal abuse. Non-police respondents confirmed the impression that verbal and psychological abuse by care-givers (family and non-family) is widespread and leaves individuals with battered self-esteem and self-confidence. Other research confirms this view (Riddington, 1989). However, police respondents did not identify these forms of victimization as a particular focus of police intervention unless they were accompanied by acts of physical violence.

Respondents with disabilities and informants from the service sector suggested that people with disabilities experience physical and sexual assault, emotional abuse and several other forms of victimization. Although not an exhaustive list of abuses experienced by people with disabilities, the following abuses are noted as being most commonly experienced by people with disabilities:

- Physical and sexual assault.

- Verbal abuse (name calling).

- Theft.[15]

- Emotional abuse (being ignored, denied personhood, systematic assaults on self-esteem and feelings of self-worth).

- Improper medical care, inappropriate ways of delivering care. Actions that are sometimes rationalized by care providers as forms of therapy, such as physical holding techniques by non-family care-givers of individuals (specifically children) with mental handicaps, were identified as abusive.

However, it is not clear whether these actions are being formally brought to the attention of the police or the broader criminal justice system as forms of violence.

- Various forms of "therapeutic treatment" (e.g., over-medication and electro-shock treatment) received in psychiatric and other care facilities. Research supports the view that abuses occur in this area (Hudson, in Hanmer and Maynard, 1987; Macdonald in Burstow and Weitz, 1988; Sager in Browne, Connors and Stern, 1985). Some analysts have drawn comparisons between actions Amnesty International defines as torture and the aversive conditioning procedures that are sometimes used as "treatment" by care-givers to control the behaviour of clients with disabilities (Stainton in The Roeher Institute, 1988). Aversive procedures include slapping, pinching, spraying water in the face, injecting lemon juice into the mouth, high volume white noise, immersion in cold water, forced body movements and other highly unpleasant controls. Police respondents for this study did not indicate that such acts by care-givers had been brought to their attention as forms of violence.

- Self-abuse such as self-mutilation and suicide attempts.

- Financial abuse (i.e., not allowing persons to have control over their own finances or abusing the trust invested in care-givers with respect to financial matters).

- Systemic violence, including failure to provide care or services that would be made available to other persons; withholding educational or employment opportunities.

- Decisions made on the individual's behalf.

- Forced participation in the production of pornography.

Victims

Police respondents had the general impression that the people with disabilities most likely to come to the attention of police as victims of violence tended to have an intellectual disability. Some of these individuals could be clearly classified as having a mental handicap, others were seen as having a learning or cognitive disability. People with mental health problems were also identified by police respondents as among those with disabilities who are more likely than others to be on the police caseload as victims.

Police respondents recalled particular instances of victimization of people with hearing, speech, mobility, agility and visual impairments. However, such incidents seemed to be rare — as far as police awareness went. Yet respondents with disabilities, family members and those from the service sector suggested that instances of victimization of people with these types of disabilities were fairly frequent, if not common. Many instances known to these people, however, were not reported to the police.

One police department confirmed that 20 of its approximately 15,000 annual complaints were made by way of Telephone Devices for the Deaf (TDDs). Because this is only .1 per cent of all complaints for that department, it was perhaps natural that the respondent was not concerned about the reporting pattern. However, a 1986 Statistics Canada survey on disability[16] showed that only .03 per cent of the entire adult Canadian public used TDDs. Of that group, .02 per cent are in Ontario urban centres outside of Toronto, where the department in question happens to be located. Therefore, that particular department was fielding between three and five times the number of complaints than perhaps would be anticipated according to the number of TDD users.[17] This detail raises an important question: those who use technology to overcome communication barriers are complaining to police departments at a higher than average rate. What, then, is happening to individuals who can neither lip-read nor sign, or who face other barriers to communication (e.g., persons with limited communication due to a cognitive disability)?

In terms of gender, females with disabilities were seen by police respondents as more likely to be victimized than their male counterparts. Some respondents, however, said that males are increasingly disclosing incidents in which they have been victimized.

The research found no clear pattern in the age of victims known to the police. One police respondent indicated that children younger than 13 were most commonly victimized, another that it was people in their early teens to mid-thirties. Most respondents saw the age pattern for victimization as essentially the same as for the population at large. However, others seemed to be aware, in particular, of criminal activity affecting senior citizens with disabilities.[18]

Increasing numbers of adults with disabilities are bringing to police attention forms of abuse alleged to have happened to them early in their lives. This trend mirrors a broader social trend where people in all facets of society are disclosing incidents of abuse. However, without police statistical data there is no way of knowing whether people with disabilities are more or less likely than others to come forward in this way, or are more or less likely to be abuse survivors.[19]

Police respondents did not generally have a clear idea about the income level of victims with disabilities. Yet those who indicated having a significant amount of contact with disabled victims felt that victims tended to be either poor or from lower middle income situations. This view is consistent with broad demographic data. Adults with disabilities are more likely than others to be poor and children with disabilities are more likely than non-disabled children to be members of poor families (Statistics Canada, 1992).

It is important to emphasize that police information is sketchy on the prevalence and forms of violence against people with disabilities. It is also sketchy on the victims. Police statistics on these issues are unavailable.[20] This problem is a direct result of a number of factors identified and discussed in more detail in Chapter 6.

Chapter 3

Perpetrators and Risk Factors

What do the police know about the perpetrators of violent acts against people with disabilities? In what situations are people at greater risk of victimization and what factors can be identified as contributing to risk? This section examines these questions.

Perpetrators

According to the police, perpetrators are usually someone known to the victim. Because victims tend to be female, perpetrators typically include fathers, brothers, uncles, grandfathers, husbands and boyfriends of single mothers. Police respondents reported that friends and neighbours victimize individuals with disabilities as do co-residents in nursing homes, rooming houses and group homes. People with mental health problems who live on the streets are seen as most likely to be victimized by someone they know and who shares street life with them.

Police respondents indicated that persons other than family members and acquaintances contribute to the violent victimization of individuals with disabilities, though to a lesser extent. Service providers identified as perpetrators included teachers, social workers, group home staff, staff in sheltered work settings, counsellors at children's centres, special transportation providers and cab drivers.

Less frequently identified by police as perpetrators were attendant care providers and providers of homemaker services. In contrast, individuals with disabilities, other respondents and researchers have indicated that vulnerability to various forms of abuse occurs in the relationships and in places where such forms of service are provided.[21] In addition, some respondents working in the social service sector said they are alarmed by the number of calls they receive regarding victimization in various settings where service providers are involved. They reported that many of these calls are probably not brought to police attention. Instead they are dealt with exclusively as social service issues.

None of the police respondents knew of instances where perpetrators were care-givers in psychiatric facilities, hospitals or multi-service institutions for persons with a mental handicap. However, research shows that people in these settings are particularly at risk and that professionals and other care-givers working in these environments may be perpetrators (Hoefkens and Allen, 1990; Nibert et al., 1989; Rabb and Rindfleisch, 1985; Blatt, 1980; Musick, 1984; Newbern, 1989).[22] Individuals who have disabilities and persons working in the social service sector interviewed for this research underscored the point that victimization frequently occurs in these environments. Several of these respondents mentioned the prevalence of abuse by staff in a variety of service and residential settings as well as abuse between residents or patients, particularly in group homes and psychiatric facilities.

Risk Factors

a. Disability

Police respondents recognized that factors inherent in having a particular disability can place individuals at higher than usual risk of victimization. For example, limited mobility can make it difficult for an individual to escape a physically or sexually abusive perpetrator. A perpetrator may regard the white cane of a blind person as a sign of that person's vulnerability to attack.

People with a cognitive disability were identified by police respondents as particularly vulnerable. Several police respondents identified factors inherent in a cognitive disability that increase vulnerability, including:

- the victim's limited understanding of and exposure to information and education on appropriate social interactions;

- limited exposure to and understanding of information on human sexuality;

- limited ability to distinguish right from wrong and, therefore, a limited grasp of the illicit or harmful nature of what the perpetrator is doing to them;

- limited understanding of what to do and who to turn to in the event of victimization;

- limited understanding of human rights and criminal justice protection, remedies and processes;

- limited ability to clearly communicate the particulars of incidents in which victimization has occurred.

It was recognized by police that difficulties in communicating may be a problem for victims with severe psychiatric problems as well. These persons may also be vulnerable because of disorientation or confusion caused by their condition or by side-effects of medication.

b. Reliance on Others

Police and other respondents identified the social context in which people with disabilities often find themselves as a major contributor to their vulnerability. For example, many individuals rely on others for intimate personal care such as bathing, using the toilet or dressing. Such personal support services are provided in a variety of situations, all of which were identified by police respondents, individuals with disabilities, and those in the social service sector or in research studies as associated with increased risk of victimization (Berkman, 1984-86; Cole, 1984-86; Sobsey and Varnhagen, 1988; Stimpson and Best, 1991). These situations include special education programming, therapy and rehabilitation programs, special housing programs with a disability-related service delivery component, institutional care facilities (including psychiatric and other hospitals), nursing or low-level care homes, and group homes for individuals with psychological and cognitive disabilities. Not to be overlooked, however, is the victim's own home, in which a personal attendant or a family member could be both care provider and perpetrator. In fact, research has shown that the sheer number of care-givers often involved in an individual's life can compound the vulnerability (Stimpson and Best, 1991).

c.   *Compliance and the Lack of Power*

Both police and non-police respondents pointed out that individuals receiving support from others are often caught in a power differential. Their lack of power in the relationship with care providers leaves individuals vulnerable.

Statistics show how reliant people with disabilities can be on others. For example, 13.2 per cent of individuals with difficulties in the area of learning or memory, and 14.1 per cent of individuals who are limited in their activities because of an emotional or psychological difficulty, are in situations where they are dependent on others for personal care.[23] They may have their finances completely managed by others (34.2 per cent and 33.1 per cent respectively). They may have their meal preparation managed entirely by others (32.4 per cent and 37.1 per cent) and may in effect be told when to eat and what to eat. Care providers may also set limits on the time and frequency people with disabilities can associate with others in the community and on their activities. In this way, individuals are either socialized to be compliant or compliance is forced upon them. Clearly, unscrupulous care providers have ample room to take advantage of people trapped in this type of situation.

The question of the power differential can become complex when the individual who requires support has an absolutely "non-negotiable" need for that support and has to rely on a perpetrator. This might be the case when, without assistance to move from the bed or wheelchair to the toilet, the individual could sustain kidney damage from prolonged urine retention. A person who requires help eating may face going hungry for days on end (particularly on the weekend) if assistance is not in place. An individual with significant intellectual limitations may need assistance with a range of activities, without which they would be unable to cope with the routine demands of daily living.

Of the nearly 1.7 million adults with disabilities who require assistance from others in daily living activities, 67.7 per cent are not getting the help they need.[24] The waiting lists for disability-related services are long. Fear of losing necessary support can tilt the power imbalance even more in favour of the perpetrator who happens to be a care provider.

d.   Ineffective Safeguards

Respondents with disabilities and others pointed out that there is no guarantee that full-time care-givers working in institutional, group home or community service organizations have been security checked. This problem has been recognized by the B. C. Ombudsman and others (Ombudsman of B.C., 1987; Docherty, 1989; McPherson, 1990). Moreover, ineffective or non-existent reporting protocols within service agencies and institutions can reinforce the impression for perpetrators that they are unlikely to be detected, which could be an added incentive to victimize others.

Non-police respondents also noted that weekend

staff working out of community agencies or in group homes are often the only care providers and sometimes the only human contact an individual with a disability might have from Friday evening to Monday morning. Yet, because these care providers are often considered part-time employees by agencies, they may not be submitted to the security checks which some full-time staff undergo. The power imbalance increases with the possibility that the care provider has a criminal past, which could include sexual or physical abuse.

Neither the issue of staff security checks nor the presence and effectiveness of reporting protocols in social and other services were identified by police respondents as contributing to the vulnerability of people with disabilities.

e. Social Isolation and the Need for Intimacy

Depending on their disability, individuals can be more or less socially isolated. A full 12.7 per cent of adults with disabilities never visit family or friends outside their own home. For people with several disabilities, that figure is 16.0 per cent. Isolated people often attach a high premium on friendship and intimacy. One police respondent described it as "competition for friendship." In these situations, the individual with a disability may confuse the role of the service provider with that of a friend — something particularly likely to happen if the individual has a cognitive disability. With that blurring of the lines, there can be confusion about what is acceptable in the relationship. Again, it can be relatively easy for the service provider to take advantage of the individual. The individual may also be reluctant to disclose what is happening if this would threaten the apparent "friendship."

In the same way, a neighbour or other acquaintance who seems to be a "friend" may turn out to be a perpetrator. But the individual's need for intimacy, perhaps poor self-image, and fear of losing an often important — perhaps the only — social interaction with someone else, could make an abusive relationship seem acceptable.

f. Individual Poverty

Several police recognized that other factors in the social situation of people with disabilities can increase the likelihood of victimization. For example, it was felt by some respondents that victims with disabilities tend to be poor or from lower income situations. This impression is supported by demographic data. People with disabilities are about twice as likely as non-disabled persons to live below the poverty line (HALS, 1986). Various research studies have linked poverty and victimization (Cash and Valentine, 1987). However, the police respondents were again sketchy on how or why poverty is a particular risk factor in the victimization of people with disabilities.

Many individuals with disabilities require disability-related services, which tend to be more readily available in urban areas. Poor people who live in urban areas are more likely to live in less affluent districts where crime rates are comparatively high. Such individuals could be at greater risk of victimization than others. They would then be at additional risk because of limitations arising directly from their disabilities.

The Hamilton-Wentworth Regional Police Service Public Safety Report (1992) shows clearly that people with disabilities are more likely than others to believe that, in their neighbourhoods, crime is on the increase. They are more likely to feel unsafe or very unsafe walking alone in their neighbourhood both day and night. They are more likely than non-disabled persons to indicate that drugs, the presence of drug dealers and intoxicated persons, and prostitution are problems in their neighbourhoods. And they are more likely to indicate that groups of people congregating in the streets, violence against women, vandalism and breaking and entering are "big problems" in their neighbourhoods. In the same way, ex-psychiatric patients who live on city streets because of a lack of affordable housing and other support services are likely to congregate in more dangerous areas, facing the same risks of victimization as other street people. This latter point was recognized by several police respondents.

g.   *Family Poverty, Stress and Turmoil*

Other social and environmental factors may place individuals at risk. Several police respondents expressed the view that many of the young persons who have intellectual disabilities, who are living with other family members and who become victimized are in unstable, low income family situations where there is turmoil, frequent moving from address to address and perhaps a family history of abuse. It was suggested, for example, that many boyfriends moving into and out of the family situation could mean additional risks.

It is statistically difficult to establish how widespread

this is. However, it is known that childhood disability is more prevalent among low than among high income families, and that the more severely disabled the child happens to be, the more likely it is that the family will be poor.[25] Poverty could be a factor behind poor maternal nutrition and health, which in turn is strongly linked with low birth weight and disability among infants (see The Canadian Institute on Child Health, *The Health of Canada's Children: A CICH Profile*, Ottawa, 1989). Then again, poverty could be a result of the limited economic mobility of families caring for children with disabilities. Such families are typically left to shoulder the entire responsibility of providing care to the disabled child, without external support services (e.g., respite services) and public funding support. In either event, children with disabilities are disproportionately represented among poor families. Researchers have established that children with disabilities are in general at greater risk than other children of abuse and maltreatment. (See Krents, Schulman and Brenner, 1987; Zantal-Weiner, 1987.) It is hardly surprising, then, that the police may be under the impression that child victims with disabilities are somewhat more likely than other child victims to come from low income situations.

In the same way, adults with disabilities who are still living at home with one or more parents are nearly twice as likely as their non-disabled counterparts to be living below the poverty line (22.7 per cent as compared with 11.8 per cent).[26] Again, family poverty in these situations could very well be related to the lack of external support available to the family care-givers. This lack of support can impede upward economic mobility. Over one-third of these nearly 42,000 poor adults living with their family of origin (36.4 per cent) indicate that they need more help with daily living activities than they are presently receiving. It is reasonable to assume that many are in family situations where their parents and perhaps siblings are "over-stressed care givers" (Schilling and Schinke, 1984). Moreover, only 59 per cent of disabled adults still living with one or both parents, and who are living below the poverty line, reside in the same home as they did five years ago.

Statistical data do suggest, then, that people with disabilities living with their parents are more likely than others to be in family situations characterized by poverty and, where there is poverty, by change. It is therefore likely that a significant proportion of disabled child abuse victims would find themselves in such circumstances.

h. Economic Dependency

Many women with disabilities find themselves in a situation of economic dependency — a factor that was recognized by police and other respondents as making them vulnerable to violence. Like other women who are living with spouses or common-law partners and who are poor, or who have no means of providing for their own economic support, women with disabilities may feel they have no option but to remain in an abusive relationship. Female spouses and common-law partners with disabilities are much more likely (37.1 per cent) than their non-disabled counterparts (17.2 per cent) to be in situations where the global family income from all sources is less than $20,000 annually.

Women with disabilities are more likely to feel economically trapped in a situation with a spouse who is violent than are non-disabled women. Only 30.9 per cent of wives and female common-law partners with disabilities have jobs, as compared with 59.3 per cent of their non-disabled counterparts. Female spouses with disabilities are over twice as likely as their non-disabled counterparts to indicate that they have never had a job or that they have been out of the labour force for two years or more.

With all these factors taken together, police respondents had a "collective awareness" of who victimizes people with disabilities. That is, it was possible to piece together the finding that the police recognize perpetrators to be people who are usually known to the victims, and that perpetrators can include family members and acquaintances, as well as various service providers as well. Similarly, a few police respondents had some insight into the risk factors that can increase the likelihood of victimization.

It must be said, however, that only a few police respondents had much insight into such matters. Any awareness at all of who victimizes people with disabilities, and why, tended to revolve around a few incidents about which the respondents had personal knowledge. It was more common for respondents to have little specific understanding of the problem, a point that was candidly admitted by several police. Moreover, the view was expressed on several occasions that the police generally have little background on these matters.

Chapter 4

Reporting Complaints

T he violent victimization of a person with a disability may be reported to the police by the victim, or by the victim's family member(s), a neighbour, friend or service provider. This chapter looks at the process for making a complaint. It also looks at the issues that victims with disabilities and the police encounter with regard to making a complaint.

Direct Complaints

Police respondents indicated that individuals with a mobility or agility limitation can make a direct complaint to the police by telephone, or they can arrange to go to the police station and make their complaint in person. This study found that efforts are being made, particularly in newer police facilities, to ensure that the premises are accessible. Older buildings may present access problems and it may be difficult to move about within them. But, as one police respondent indicated, "One way or another, we'll get them in the building."

An individual may be unable to come directly to the police station and may be in a potentially dangerous situation. In these cases, police respondents reported, some departments arrange to have the person removed to a safe location to make the complaint if this is requested or seems an obvious need. Alternatively, the police have the authority to remove the perpetrator from the situation to enable the victim to make his or her complaint.

Individuals with a hearing or speech impairment can follow much the same procedure in making a complaint. If telephone use is a problem, they may have the option of calling the police on a Telephone Device for the Deaf (TDD). Although it seems fairly common for police communication centres — the units that respond to incoming calls — to have TDDs, it is not universal. Complainants can also call the police using the relay (interpreter) service provided by telephone companies. Several police respondents indicated that their departments have communicated with victims this way.

Individuals with a hearing or speaking impairment may find that the police department has sign language interpreters on staff.[27] If this is not the case, the department may have links with agencies providing these services in the community. The department may also have links with organizations and individuals able to understand other forms of communication, such as Bliss symbols. Respondents generally indicated that the police are willing to arrange for whatever services are needed, and will cover any costs involved.

In addition, the police department may have links to multicultural organizations which are able to provide interpreter services for individuals whose mother tongue is not English. Some of these agencies are able to mediate communication for victims who use sign language or who have limited communication because of a cognitive disability. However, it is not clear how many multicultural agencies have this capacity.

Where a complainant has a cognitive disability or seems confused for other reasons, several police respondents indicated that the department will dispatch an officer to meet the person and hear their complaint. If an individual wants to come to the police station but is uncertain about how to do so (perhaps because of lack of familiarity with bus routes), an officer may be dispatched. It is not clear, however, how commonly this is done.

Some respondents indicated there may be some risk that police would not dispatch a patrol officer when needed. A large proportion of all complaints to the police turn out to be either false alarms or about matters that are not serious. Therefore, police departments are increasingly implementing priority response schemes to effectively manage scarce resources. Under these arrangements, complaints about serious matters such as sexual assault would automatically trigger the dispatch of a patrol officer. The response for less serious matters would be delayed or even deferred altogether (e.g., bicycle theft, where the person would be invited to visit the police station and fill out a report). Some police respondents conjectured that there may be a small risk of delayed response or non-response to a serious matter where telephone complainants were unable to make themselves clearly understood. Whether significant problems will actually arise in this area remains to be seen. Generally, however, the police seem to operate on the premise that at the slightest hint that a complainant is attempting to tell about a serious matter, the police have an obligation to respond.

In many ways, then, the perception of police is that facilities and the procedures for making direct complaints to the police are for the most part accessible to people with various disabilities. Where accessibility may be a problem, police respondents at least indicated an active interest in doing whatever is necessary to enable people with disabilities to make their complaints.

Indirect Complaints

Many complaints are not made directly by victims, but by friends, neighbours, family members or service providers such as teachers, social workers, attendant care providers, homemakers, schools for the deaf, sheltered work program staff or group home staff. The informants may have clear evidence that some form of abuse occurred (e.g., they saw it happen) or may simply suspect that something is wrong (e.g., an aunt who visits infrequently notices a radical and disturbing personality change in her niece with a disability). Some respondents indicated that a high proportion of complaints involving victims with cognitive disabilities and psychological difficulties are made this way.

The procedure for indirect complaints is straightforward: the complaint can be made by telephone, by direct visit to the police station or by correspondence. Some departments assign officers to work with the community by participating on various committees. These officers could be informed about violence affecting people with disabilities through these channels.

The police may become aware of victimization while investigating another matter. For example, the police may field a call about wife assault. Once at the residence where the alleged incident is occurring, the patrol officer may detect a child with a disability who is unusually disturbed and has suspicious-looking bruises. The officer may suspect abuse and pursue the matter. In other instances, an investigator's questioning may lead an individual to disclose incidentally that they or someone they know had been victimized. That disclosure would likely be pursued.

The police have widely implemented protocols for fielding complaints about child victimization brought to their attention by child welfare workers such as Children's Aid Society (CAS) workers. In fact, these social workers have a legal responsibility to report family violence to the police where it is suspected under the *Child and Family Services Act*, Revised Statutes, Ontario 1990, c11 s72(a). The protocols aim to ensure collaboration between the police and child welfare workers from the time the complaint is made until the completion of the criminal investigation. Children with disabilities would be included among the victims covered under these protocols. However, none of the police informants indicated that these protocols specifically say how CAS workers and police officers are to proceed in the event that a child with a disability has been victimized.

There are similar protocols concerning relations between the police and the school system in reference to child abuse. One police respondent expressed the view, however, that educators have concerns about confidentiality and may not be bringing to police attention as many incidents as are actually occurring or suspected. Again, schools and the police seem to negotiate specific considerations relating to the student's disability on a discretionary, case-by-case, basis rather than having them set down formally in the protocol guidelines.

Other protocols such as those relating to senior abuse are being developed by some departments. While many senior citizens have disabilities, it is unclear how widely specific disability-related requirements and considerations will be set out in the protocols.

Hospitals and mental health facilities have reporting protocols.[28] However, protocols are not universally in place in the social service sector. Protocols relating to police response to complaints made by social service agencies or institutional care facilities do not seem to be widely in place. Several police informants pointed out that, where communication with these agencies and institutions has been considered at all, the protocols are informal.

None of the police respondents indicated that their police department has a protocol specifically on how to handle calls about the victimization of people with disabilities. The general pattern is for people with disabilities to be included in other police protocols, despite the fact that these protocols are either informal or, if formalized, do not have guidelines specific to disability issues.

Issues Concerning Complaint-making

a. The Lack of Protocols to Link Police and Other Agencies

The absence of protocols relating to handling complaints concerning victims with disabilities may be a problem. On one hand, it is legitimate to ask whether yet another protocol should be added to an already complex police regulatory environment, and whether such a protocol would actually be useful. Where the police have informal working links with community agencies, respondents think these arrangements are working effectively. On the other hand, it is difficult to see how the policing system as a whole can equitably respond to the complaints of victims with disabilities in the absence of some guidelines. Without clear guidelines and procedures, much is left to the sensitivity of individual officers to victims with disabilities. A great deal is left to individual police knowledge about what steps can be taken and who to turn to for assistance. And without system-wide guidelines, the inclination of particular departments and officers to take an active approach to detecting victimization becomes all the more crucial.

In larger urban settings, support services such as sign language interpreters are likely to be available to help victims make their complaints. The research found that it is fairly common for the police to have working links with these agencies. However, it was also found that there may be delays in securing such services in rural and smaller urban settings. One police respondent said these services were not in place at all in his particular region. In one case, this gap in community

45

service not only made it difficult for a deaf victim to make a complaint, but proved frustrating for the victim and officers during the investigation.

b. Under-reporting: Effects of Fear and Control

Several police respondents indicated that it would be difficult for an individual who is severely mobility impaired (e.g., bed-ridden) and who is being victimized to make a direct complaint. It was recognized that a perpetrator could simply prevent the victim from using the telephone. In this situation, the police would not know about the incident unless it was reported by others. Without knowledge of the incident, obviously the police are unable to do anything about it. In the same way, an individual in a highly controlling service environment such as a group home or institution may be prevented by a care-giver-perpetrator from using the telephone. It would be left to other staff or co-residents to report the incident. Yet there are pressures and disincentives that could prevent these persons from reporting the incident (Berkman, 1984-86; Maibaum, 1985).

These issues point to the critical need for family members, neighbours and service-providing staff to be aware of the signs of victimization, to know what to do in that event and to have some incentive to report the problem to the police. In fact, several police respondents said they rely heavily on these persons for information about the victimization of individuals with disabilities who are "captive" to their perpetrators.

The research found other reasons for under-reporting. Many people with disabilities are socialized to be compliant with the disability service system. They may even fear care providers, many of whom may be seen as authority figures. A young woman with a disability who has been socialized this way, and who has been sexually abused, would have to overcome many inhibitions before finding the courage to bring the matter to police attention. Approaching the police could be intimidating in itself. Armed and uniformed officers are, after all, quite widely seen as icons of power and authority.

One police respondent suggested that the police establish a presence in the community that neither looks nor feels like a police station, for example a community agency that provides counselling services. The conjecture was that a less formal and less intimidating point of contact with the police may help victims overcome some of the inhibitions that would keep them from disclosing their victimization.

It was found through interviews with people with disabilities that they often feel they are simply not listened to by others or, if they are, the listener tends to be dismissive, unbelieving or impatient. An adult with a cognitive disability or psychological difficulty, for example, who is repeatedly dealt with as if he is either an incompetent person or a child, may have the perception that he would not be believed if he were to complain to the police about being victimized. If this person were to report despite these obstacles, and were dealt with insensitively or dismissively by the police, it would be unlikely that he would report again should there be further victimization.

Some police respondents reported that a parent may not want to know about the abuse of his or her child and may dismiss or suppress the disabled child's complaint. The example was given of a mother who denied her disabled daughter's allegation that she was being sexually abused by her step-father. This problem becomes all the more difficult if the child has limited communication skills and is therefore reliant on the parent to inform the police.

Fear about others knowing of the abuse was identified as another factor that discourages victims from reporting to the police. The young woman with a cognitive disability who fears that her parents would be upset if they knew she had been sexually abused may be afraid to tell them or the police about the incident. The psychiatric patient, residential care client, group home resident or receiver of attendant services who is worried about care-giver reprisal may not tell anyone about his or her victimization to protect his or her own safety. The street person or person living in a lodging house may fear reprisal by the perpetrator if a complaint is made — particularly if charges are not laid or the case is dismissed.

c. *Under-reporting: Internal Reporting Procedures (Social and Other Services)*

Some police respondents believe that group homes, institutions and other care-providing agencies usually have their own internal processes for fielding victim complaints. Complaints do not come to police attention because, they conjectured, issues are being effectively dealt with by the social service, health and mental health systems. To some extent this view was backed by informants working in the social service sector. A psychiatric facility may, for example, have a protocol for reporting the alleged abuse of residents. Many complaints would be dealt with as a staff discipline matter. In this way, violence against people with disabilities is effectively decriminalized; criminal issues are dealt with as social service and staffing issues. This problem has been identified in other research (Musick, 1984).

At the same time, it is crucial to point out that these internal procedures are not universally in place in the social service sector.[29] During this research it was found that one social service agency implemented an administrative protocol only after a care provider — a group home staff person — had allegedly abused several of the agency's clients. Here, guidelines for reporting were developed and implemented only after a crisis had emerged. In another instance, it was found that a group home staff person had been allegedly sexually abusing one of his disabled clients. The employing agency had no administrative procedures for dealing with the matter. That particular organization continues to operate without such a mechanism, though the allegation was never dropped. "They don't want to know ..." commented one respondent.

These incidents raise an important question that has direct implications for people with disabilities and reporting of their victimization: what are the incentives for social service agencies and institutional care facilities to report? One police respondent conjectured that care-providing agencies may be concerned about damaging their own reputation to the point that they suppress information they should bring to police attention.

Other police informants believe that serious social and legal pressures have already been put on the administrators of social service and health agencies[30] to disclose known incidents of victimization. They believe that, because of this pressure, administrators are bringing incidents of victimization of people with disabilities to police attention. It was then surmised that, because the overall volume of complaints from this sector is negligible, violent victimization in social service settings is not a significant problem. However, interviews conducted for this research, and other research studies, point towards a different conclusion: incidents are occurring in the social service sector but, for various reasons, they are being suppressed or dealt with as non-criminal, staffing issues.

This again raises important questions about the mechanisms and protocols for liaison between police and social service agencies. It raises questions about how effective and active police approaches to crime detection would look in these circumstances. It also raises questions about legislation and policy governing the social service sector and about the efficacy of government monitoring and enforcement.

d. Attitudes of Officers

The attitude of the officer who takes a complaint may also inhibit a victim from fully disclosing details of an incident and could prevent further police response. One respondent in the disability-related service sector explained that a resident of a particular institutional facility had attempted to report a complaint to the police. However, because of the complainant's diagnosed condition, the officer assumed the person could not provide meaningful information. Not only was no investigation undertaken, the complaint was not fully heard.

A number of people with disabilities, as well as respondents from the disability-related service sector, noted that police officers tended to address service providers rather than talking directly to the person who has a disability. For example, in the presence of both the person with a disability who has been victimized and a non-disabled service provider, a police officer might ask the service provider, "Does she know at what time this incident occurred?" rather than asking the individual herself. This seems to be the experience particularly of people with mental and cognitive disabilities and with speech impairments. The failure to respect and acknowledge the person can result in further feelings of victimization.

In the present study, it is not possible to determine the prevalence of these problems. However, police respondents reported that police officers are no less likely to harbour stereotypes and lack awareness about people with disabilities than is the rest of the population.[31]

Similarly, civilian complaint-takers in police communication centres may lack awareness about disability. This can create problems for victims who are attempting to make complaints. Civilian complaint-takers are common at police stations. These persons do not undergo the same basic and in-service training as police officers — training that has traditionally had only a minimal focus on disability in any event. As a result, complaint-takers may simply not understand that the telephone complainant who sounds intoxicated may actually have slurred speech due to cerebral palsy or medications. The person who sounds inarticulate may be hard of hearing, which in turn affects speech. The person who sounds disoriented and perhaps disinterested in making an intelligible complaint may be having difficulties reporting because of severe psychological depression, a cognitive limitation, or the side-effects of psycho-active medications. The complainant who seems to have a bizarre manner may have a multiple personality or some other personality disorder, or may have a condition such as Tourette's Syndrome. It was not clear to police respondents whether complaint-takers have been sensitized to such issues.

In many ways, then, the police are open to receiving complaints concerning people with disabilities who have been victimized. They are making efforts to ensure their facilities and procedures are accessible. On the other hand, it seems highly probable that incidents of victimization are significantly under-reported by people with disabilities. Factors that have been identified as affecting complaint-making include: the absence of protocols to guide relations between police and care-givers; the absence of services and informal supports for potential complainants in some communities (such as sign language interpreters); care providers' power over more severely disabled individuals to prevent or inhibit disclosure; the victim's deeply ingrained sense that the police will probably not believe him; the victim's fear about what will happen if family members or care providers find out about the disclosure; internal protocols in some institutions that may simply screen incidents and prevent them from coming to police attention; social pressures in the social and institutional services that inhibit co-workers of perpetrators from reporting; fear on the part of care-providing agencies about their own reputations in the event of victim disclosure; the attitude of the individual officer; and lack of knowledge about disability on the part of complaint-takers.

Chapter 5

The Initial Police Response to Complaints

P olice respondents for this research consistently indicated that, once the police have received a complaint concerning the individual with a disability — or any other person — who has been violently victimized, they will investigate. None of the police who were interviewed for this study indicated that the police have any option *but* to investigate in such circumstances. Whether or not a victim has a disability is irrelevant to that basic police obligation. Police respondents further indicated that the police investigation would, especially where violence is involved, run its full course like any other investigation. Investigations proceed according to standard procedures until the officers are convinced that they have obtained all relevant evidence. Other than adjusting the questioning and mode of communication to the victim's particular abilities and needs, there is no "special" method of investigation concerning individuals with disabilities who have been victimized.

Another general point was raised about the tenor and thoroughness of investigations. Some police reported that it is "only human nature" for investigators to feel a heightened empathy towards victims who are particularly vulnerable to their perpetrators. This would include children, senior citizens and individuals with disabilities. The view was expressed that police officers tend to "bend over backwards" in these situations to make sure they do a thorough job. Yet it was also emphasized that these investigations would proceed essentially the same as other investigations.

Victim Consent to Police Involvment

Where a complaint is made by someone other than the victim and compelling evidence to lay a criminal charge is not available at the outset of the case, some respondents reported that the police will determine whether the victim wants to pursue the matter. Does the victim want the police to be involved? If not, there may not be much more the police can do about the matter until the victim indicates otherwise or unless compelling evidence is delivered to the police.

Establishing Safety and Trust

According to the police respondents, the typical police response early in an investigation is to try to ensure the victim's safety and comfort. This may involve moving the complainant to a safe place such as the police station, a hotel room or some other, usually non-public, place of the victim's choice. Some police respondents said they had arranged for victims with disabilities to be moved to safe environments and that in some instances special transportation and support service arrangements such as attendant care had to be made. As mentioned earlier, the perpetrator could also be removed from the situation and kept in police custody, but usually only for a brief period unless there was sufficient evidence to lay charges.

The police respondents suggested that they would, at the outset of a case, make an effort to establish a rapport with the victim and to build a bond of trust. On one level this was seen as simply a humane and compassionate response — the morally "right" thing to do. On another level, establishing a bond of trust is crucial to building the criminal case. The more comfortable the victim feels in disclosing what happened and the clearer his story, the more evidence the police will have to draw upon in constructing a case.

The study found that, where the police have investigated incidents involving victims with disabilities, several strategies are pursued to help victims feel comfortable. People with whom victims feel safe and receive personal support, such as a sister, friend or mother, may be included in the investigation.[32] It may be important for the investigators to be plainclothes rather than uniformed officers. In some departments all investigators are plainclothes officers. According to the police respondents, if the victim would feel more comfortable with a female investigator, efforts would probably be made to involve one. If this could not be arranged, a female victim assistance worker would be brought in to provide support.

Police respondents noted that, in situations where the victim is too traumatized to communicate, the investigator may return the next day or perhaps several days later. If the victim is able only to disclose fragments of the story at a time, several visits might be required to piece together the entire story. Some police respondents indicated that it is not uncommon to visit a victim many times over several months. It may even be weeks before the victim feels comfortable enough to begin disclosing the particulars of the incident.

Police efforts to establish the victim's safety and trust are becoming routine policing procedures regardless of disability. However, some respondents reported that police have used these approaches for victims with disabilities in particular. It is not possible in the present study to determine how extensively the latter is actually occurring.

Arranging Supports

The research found that, where victims have limited communication skills, or communicate using sign language or symbols, the police have, in some instances, brought into investigations individuals who can help mediate the communication. Such services include sign language interpreters and Bliss symbol interpreters. Special transportation and other measures to accommodate victims during investigations and court proceedings have also been made.

It would appear that it is more common for the police in larger urban areas — where support services are more likely to be in place[33] — to make these arrangements than in less densely populated areas. Some respondents indicated that their departments had covered the associated costs, and that the costs had not posed significant problems during investigations. Some police indicated that the Crown attorney had been particularly helpful in making these arrangements. However, other respondents indicated that these supports were not, at least to their knowledge, available in their communities at all. It was generally felt that, if the victim can communicate effectively — even if they have to use a symbol system or interpreter — the victim's disability will not usually present insurmountable problems for investigators or courts of law.

It is not clear whether victims are satisfied with the communication and other disability-related supports the police arranged during investigations. There is a lack of formal evaluation procedures on this issue.[34]

Issues Concerning the Initial Police Response

a. Obtaining Assistance from Others

Although police respondents were generally willing to ensure the support the victim requires is arranged, they reported that investigations can be questionable on several counts. First, the perpetrator may be someone who would normally provide important support to the victim such as personal care or communication assistance. Police apprehension and detention of the perpetrator in this instance may involve the virtual collapse of the victim's support system.

Arranging community support for victims with disabilities can involve a time lag. Arranging for sign language interpreters is a case in point. In the words of one informant, "They're not exactly sitting around waiting for a call from the police." Then again, the community may be unable to provide support services because they do not exist or because the community is over-burdened with demand. Another police respondent suggested that the police should anticipate problems arranging support and have well-thought-out contingency plans. That respondent asked, "If plan A doesn't work, what's plan B?"

The ability of the police to arrange for assistance during the investigation depends in large part on how well informed they are about community resources. To that end, police departments may maintain registries on helpful community services and experts who can be brought into the investigative process.

However, whether such registries remain current will depend largely on the police keeping them updated. It will also depend on whether community agencies and organizations keep the police informed about new supports and services. Some police were sceptical about whether their particular registries were current. One informant said candidly that their particular department does not have such a registry and that the department would not know where to turn for various kinds of assistance. Others said their departments have registries. However, they said, they personally have a sketchy understanding about which disability-related organizations are operating in their area and the role they could play in the investigative process. The information contained in the registries does not seem to be disseminated within the police department or perhaps is not seen as useful.

Despite the apparent desire and good will of officers to "do what's right," then, it should not be assumed at present that they are aware of who in the community can provide assistance during the investigation of incidents in which people with disabilities have been victimized.

The design of the registries and information systems on disability-related and other community resources seems to be left to the discretion of individual departments. No doubt some departments have better approaches than others to obtaining and organizing such information. These approaches could in turn serve as models for other departments. However, police respondents generally indicated that they were not aware of what other departments were doing in terms of disability-related information management.

The willingness of other members of the community to assist in investigations was also raised as a problem area. Respondents specifically mentioned the reluctance of some medical doctors to become involved in the process. The investigation and, if the case proceeds to court, the trial proceedings could involve several days of a physician's time. It was observed that physicians are not always willing to get involved in investigations with significant time commitments. The police may be left "doctor shopping," in the words of one respondent.

The police may encounter another dilemma with community agencies. In the victimization of someone in a facility, the professional opinion of the facility's psychiatrist might be sought on the emotional and behaviour patterns of the alleged victim. But there may be implicit or explicit pressure on that expert not to divulge particular information, especially if it might implicate facility staff. The same could be true about the administrator of the local group home agency or attendant care service. On the one hand, the police may need to rely on social service, health, mental health providers and educators for assistance during investigations, and, on the other hand, those are systems in which victimization can and does occur. The assistance provided to police may therefore be biased in favour of alleged perpetrators in the interests of saving face.

Even obtaining assistance from other members of the police department may be a problem. Many departments have a victim services or a victim assistance program. Civilian and police workers in these programs either provide support that victims require such as counselling or arrange for others in the community to provide the support. However, not all departments have these programs. One respondent indicated that the victim assistance coordinator position at that particular department was funded on a contract basis and the funding had been recently cut. "Now there is a major gap in the area of victim assistance," the respondent noted.

b. Professional Manner

Although the research found that police are becoming increasingly aware of the need for sensitivity in questioning victims, it was found that traditional policing practice and training have left their imprint. Despite police efforts, non-police respondents suggested that victims still sometimes find investigating officers abrupt in their manner or style of questioning. This perception, in turn, can make the victim feel inhibited about disclosing.

In the same way, investigators by necessity have a professional concern with uncovering the facts. Understandably, they may want to get at the particulars of an incident as efficiently as possible. However, the victim may not share this interest in efficiency. Victims may, because of their disability or because of the trauma they undergo, have a round-about way of reporting the incident. In other cases, the victim may see the investigating officer as the first person to show any interest in what may be a life punctuated by victimization.

Some police reported that they had encountered victims with disabilities who had discursive communication styles and family histories of victimization. It would perhaps be natural for these victims to begin telling the full story — from the very beginning. Yet it was recognized that victims may feel officers becoming impatient. The victims can lose trust and stop telling their stories, which in turn affects investigations. This would seem to be a general hazard of police investigations. It is not clear how often this occurs in cases involving victims with disabilities. However, there is no reason why victims with disabilities would be any less affected than others by the professional demeanour and style of officers. The next chapter of this study points to a number of factors that can make the victim with a disability feel all the more apprehensive during the investigative process.

c. *Officer Knowledge About, or Prior Contact with, People with Disabilities*

It was found during the research that police officers have little, if any, contact with people with disabilities. New recruit training has not focused on disability issues in any significant way. Neither has in-service training on "victim sensitivity" or community trends made disability a major focus of attention. Therefore, police officers are generally no better informed about, or sensitive to, disability issues than the rest of the population.

Police respondents themselves pointed out that officers may have the same stereotypical and prejudicial attitudes as the rest of the community. It is true that officers have been trained in the importance of setting personal biases aside while policing. Yet this begs the question: what personal biases should be set aside if the officer is not even familiar with the more common disability stereotypes? Does the officer assume that, because the individual has a disability, they are less likely than others to be victimized? Does the officer assume that, because a person has a particular disability, he is incapable of telling what happened to him or that he is probably making things up? Does the officer assume that, because the individual has severe, and perhaps several, disabilities, she somehow lacks the same range of feelings or memories as others? Does the officer know that the vast majority of people with disabilities live in regular neighbourhoods, not in "safe" institutions? Clearly, lack of background on disability issues that affect policing leaves officers less well equipped than they might be to respond effectively to people with disabilities when they happen to become victims of violence.

On the other hand, police officers may have been called upon to socially control people in certain segments of the disabled community. This kind of involvement could, in turn, entrench particular views on disability. For example, officers are trained in dealing with persons causing a disturbance who might fall under the jurisdiction of the *Mental Health Act*. Here, the police role may be to establish control over the persons and to persuade them to commit themselves to a mental health facility or to undergo a psychiatric assessment. For the officer this involvement could entail some risk of personal injury. At other times officers may be called to locate and control individuals who are severely disoriented, perhaps due to the effects of psycho-active medications.

Officers may also be called upon to establish control of individuals labelled mentally handicapped who are living in group home settings and who are acting aggressively towards one another or towards group home staff. One police respondent indicated that their police department had "more than its share" of this kind of involvement. In these instances, the focus of police attention on people with disabilities (to the degree that there is any focus) would be confined to disturbed and perhaps violent persons involved in unsavoury incidents and who perhaps present risks to themselves or others, including officers.

One can only guess at how such experiences, if these are officers' primary experiences with the disabled community, would affect policing attitudes and sensitivities. Moreover, during a literature review conducted for this study it was found that a great deal of the scholarly research on the police response to people with disabilities has focused on people with disabilities as perpetrators rather than as victims. In other words, the field of criminology has not presented a mass of research to counteract police biases where biases exist.

The research found, then, that police seem to consider it necessary to investigate all cases of victimization brought to their attention, regardless of whether victims have disabilities. Generally, investigations of incidents involving victims with disabilities are seen by the police to follow the same course as any other investigation. Where someone other than the victim reports the incident, victim consent to police involvement is usually sought. If the victim declines, the police may decide there is little more they can do. If, however, the victim can be made to feel comfortable and safe, they may begin telling about the incident. On the basis of the victim's disclosure, officers can begin building a case.

To assist in the process, a variety of supports for victims with disabilities can and have been arranged by the police. However, the research also found that police cannot always arrange support. This seems to be a more common problem in less densely populated areas than in large cities, although it was also found that police in urban areas encounter this problem. Moreover, the police may not know where to look for support because they do not have a registry of community services, their registries are not current or the information in the registries has not been effectively disseminated.

Other problems arise when people who may be able to assist in police investigations may not be inclined to do so, or the assistance the police obtain from various service providers in the community may be biased. In addition, officers' own personal biases, prejudices and lack of background on disability issues can affect their response to complaints, as can the professional style of officers who focus on determining the facts of the case at the expense of the victim's trust and comfort level.

Chapter 6

Building the Case

The research looked at general procedures officers follow during investigations and at key considerations they have while building cases. It was found that the police perceive difficulties in investigations particularly when victims have limited communication abilities due to cognitive disabilities or significant psychological difficulties. It was found that police investigators face other difficulties that can affect whether they will lay charges and attempt to bring cases to trial. The discussion in this chapter looks at important stages of the investigative process and issues the police have to address.

Establishing the Facts

a. The Victim's Recall

As discussed in the previous chapter, it is important to the investigation that the victim have opportunities to tell the story. On the basis of these disclosures, officers can begin constructing the particulars of the incident. Police said they had encountered problems in determining what in fact occurred during incidents involving victims with disabilities.

For example, it was reported that individuals with cognitive disabilities may simply be unable to remember clearly what happened, where it happened, when it happened and who was involved. There may be inconsistencies in a story due to the victim's confused, selective or intermittent memory. A victim may remember that an incident happened when it was cold but cannot recall whether it was in the late fall, early spring or dead of winter.

Establishing the order of events can also be a problem when individuals have problems with sequencing. Moreover, the information may not be specific — the victim may know the incident took place "in the park," but may not be able to specify which park or where in the park. A victim may indicate that she was abused more than once but be unclear about whether it happened ten times or five times. The victim's attention span could also be short, which could present problems.

These are very real challenges for the police. Clear evidence will almost certainly be required for a successful trial or a pre-trial guilty plea by the perpetrator. If investigating officers cannot muster enough evidence to solidly support the victim's complaint in a court of law, the police would be discouraged from pressing charges in the first place. Some police respondents indicated that this does happen in many cases. Effectively, victims fall through the cracks because the victims cannot provide — or are presumed by the police as unable to provide — clear and reliable evidence.

Yet one police respondent related that their department got around problems in a case involving a victim with significant cognitive and communication limitations. Investigators were able to establish that the violent incident had happened at a particular type of location (a school yard) but were unable to determine which place in particular. Based on fragments of descriptive information about the site from the victim, the investigators used their own knowledge of the area to narrow the possible locations to a few probable sites. The investigators then personally drove the victim to these sites. Eventually the victim was able to recall that "this" was the place where the incident occurred.

In this instance, the victim with significant disabilities seems to have reacted to the traumatic event essentially as a non-disabled victim might: to involuntarily suppress any memory of it. Once back where the incident took place, however, memories began to return. There is no particular reason for police to assume that, because the victim has a significant disability, that person has no memory of the traumatic event. At the same time, there is no good reason for the police to assume that the victim's apparent inability to recall is anything other than a natural psychological defence mechanism. That is, the inability to recall a profoundly traumatic event should not be interpreted as some lack of intellectual ability on the part of the victim. What may be the real issue in these instances is how investigators can elicit the initial bits of descriptive evidence and interpret them — regardless of disability — so the investigation can focus on the probable facts of the matter, instead of floundering among possibilities or winding up the case prematurely.

It is not clear how often the police actually go to these lengths, or what strategies they use to glean such fragments of descriptive information. However, the overall impression was that the police are somewhat overwhelmed by the challenge. This impression is supported by the alarmingly low proportion of cases involving perpetrators of violence against victims with disabilities in which charges are laid. (See Sobsey, 1988; and Stimpson and Best, 1991.) However, one police respondent presented the view that juries are becoming increasingly sensitive to the victimization of vulnerable persons. This respondent believed that, if a case is brought to court, juries are more likely now than previously to provide a sympathetic hearing — despite any apparent shortcomings of the victim's story. The implication is that the police should be taking advantage of this emerging public sensitivity.

b. Embellishments

A difficult issue that was identified by some police respondents is that victims may, for various reasons, embellish their stories. This may occur, it was reported, if the victim has been socialized to be compliant and has grown accustomed to satisfying the demands of power figures. Here, the victim may add details to the story to make it sound like what they think the investigating officer wants to hear.[35] Similarly, some respondents reported that the victim may feel guilty about the incident and may introduce elements to his story to deflect what he perceives would be blame. The details may not hold up under scrutiny, confuse the investigation and ultimately weaken the case.

However, the disabled victim's embellishment of a substantially correct account of a violent incident may not be the result of a subconscious desire to please investigators. The victim may simply have confused memories. For example, a person who has a psychological problem may be confused about the particulars of an incident if, at the time the event occurred, a new medication was beginning to take effect and he was disoriented. An individual who had been repeatedly victimized may be unable to mentally compartmentalize the particulars of one traumatic incident from the next. Then again, the victim would not necessarily have to be receiving medication, or to have undergone a history of abuse, or to have an intellectual disability, to confuse the particulars of a traumatic incident in which he was violently victimized.

Some police respondents consider that, if a victim's embellishments came to the attention of the defence attorney, the attorney would likely pounce on the details to discredit the victim's testimony. Sorting out what actually happened in the incident and the extraneous details injected by the victim can present a major investigative challenge. Some respondents reported that, if investigators feel that they cannot separate the wheat from the chaff in the victim's story, they may have few options but to avoid pressing charges.

Yet are police always certain that cases involving non-disabled victims will hold up in court before pressing charges, or do police live with an element of uncertainty in these cases? If the police are not always certain how cases will fare where non-disabled victims are concerned, why the disproportionately high need for certainty where victims have disabilities?

c. *Limited Communication and Contamination of Evidence*

The limited communication skills of the victim can pose significant problems for investigators. A person with limited communication skills may have developed her own idiosyncratic language to refer to people or intimate body parts. Another victim may have few if any verbal or sign language skills and may have significant difficulty communicating any pertinent details that the investigating officers could use to build a case. One police respondent indicated that investigating officers may be so uncertain about what actually happened during the victimizing incident that the police may be left wondering whether they are pressing charges for the correct offence.

Where officers are having problems understanding the idiosyncratic communication pattern of the victim, several police respondents said that they will try to obtain help from someone who understands the person, such as a friend or family member.[36] In these cases, however, the communicator is likely to have an empathic relationship with the victim, especially if the victim has been traumatized. While the empathy is natural and not a problem in itself, the respondents reported that it can lead the communicator to take liberties in interpreting the particulars of the incident. In the interests of helping the victim and getting a conviction against the alleged perpetrator, the communicator may inadvertently fill in details that they *think* the victim is trying to communicate, but which the victim is actually *not* trying to communicate. Much the same problem is faced when sign language and other language interpreters are involved in cases.

The extraneous details that communicators introduce into the victim's story can confuse the investigation. The details could be used by the defence attorney as ammunition against the credibility of the victim or the integrity of the investigation. Yet several police respondents indicated that, in anticipation of this problem, they would counsel the communicator on the importance of neither adding to nor taking away from what the victim is actually indicating.

d. Lifestyle Turmoil

The individual's social circumstances may be inherently confusing, which would simply compound the other difficulties investigators encounter. For instance, a person who has a mental health problem and who lives on the street may not care what day of the week it is because the days tend to blur together. Then the specific date that a violent act was perpetrated against her could remain open to question. In the same way, the victim may come from a family that is frequently moving, where there is turmoil in inter-personal relations, or where family routines are confused or non-existent. Here, the young victim with a disability may have difficulty remembering specific details about a violent event.

e. Victim Consistency

Another set of difficulties revolves around whether the individual's story would be consistent in the future, should the case proceed to trial. If an individual seems clear today about what happened when she was victimized, there is no guarantee that she will be able to keep the details straight three months from now, when the court will be in session. Under cross examination, will the victim garble the testimony? This is a police concern even for non-disabled victims and a particular concern regarding individuals who are prone to significant memory loss or confusion arising from their disabling condition.

Although this issue does not seem to affect the investigation of cases, respondents indicated that police officers must judge the probability of the testimony standing up in court — a judgement call that could discourage the police from laying charges. On the other hand, the researchers also heard about Crown attorneys and police who have gone out of their way to ensure that victims were able to keep the details of their stories straight.[37] Witness assistance programs have also proven helpful in this regard.

f.   Forensic and Other Evidence

Aside from attempting to gather the descriptive evidence the victim is able to provide, some respondents reported that investigators would typically seek out other evidence as well.[38] Officers might look for personal objects indicating that the perpetrator had been with the victim during the alleged incident. These might be a beer bottle with the perpetrator's finger prints or one of the perpetrator's personal possessions. Forensic evidence such as hair and semen may be sought.[39] The FBI has underscored the importance of the police making efforts to obtain forensic evidence, particularly where the victim has limited ability to communicate or where their testimony is doubted (Federal Bureau of Investigation and Metro-Dade Police Department, 1983). How widely this evidence is actually sought in cases involving victims with disabilities, however, is not clear.

The research found that, in addition to material evidence, investigators would likely attempt to determine who else knows about the particular incident, or about similar incidents involving either the victim or the alleged perpetrator. Accordingly, neighbours, friends, family members, service providers and others may be contacted and questioned.[40]

Some respondents reported that there may be reason to believe that others — perhaps co-residents of the victim's group home — may have been victimized by the same perpetrator. Here, it was reported that investigators would try to obtain "similar complaint" evidence in support of the victim's case. If the police are able to obtain that evidence, they may initiate other investigations into the incidents involving victims who made similar complaints.

A family member, a teacher or perhaps a psychologist[41] who knows the victim well may, upon questioning, indicate that the victim has undergone a significant personality change (for example, having nightmares, bed wetting or crying frequently) that roughly coincides with the timing of the alleged incident. Evidence that a significant change has occurred would again lend support to the notion that some event has traumatized the victim.

g. Police Questioning

Some police respondents reported that the questions asked by investigators, how these are asked, the officer's assumptions about the victim's abilities when framing questions and how the victim's responses are interpreted, all have a critical bearing on the police investigation. A particular question may not elicit a response from the victim or may elicit a response that is difficult to interpret. Several police respondents stressed how important it is that police officers do not dismiss anything the victim says. They commented on the importance of adopting a flexible and creative approach to the investigation and of assuming that the victim — regardless of the nature or severity of their condition — is a complete human being who has something important to tell. These respondents also commented on investigations involving victims with disabilities that went awry because officers had not adopted such approaches.

Victim Consent

Some police respondents reported that a defence attorney may make possible allegations that the victim perhaps consented to acts that they say were perpetrated against them. It can be difficult for police to prepare for this allegation. Where it is not clear whether the victim knows the difference between right and wrong, and appropriate and inappropriate touching, and where the victim's communication skills are extremely limited, showing the victim's refusal to consent becomes difficult.

If it cannot be shown that the victim was withholding consent during the incident, then the perpetrator could claim that they thought the victim was consenting. Here, the police may not feel that they have the evidence they need to press charges and bring the case to trial.

At the same time it is important to note that most people with disabilities do not have a learning or intellectual disability. They are aware of whether they have been victimized and whether they consented to a given action such as sexual intercourse. In fact, many, if not most, people who do happen to have cognitive disabilities also have this awareness. The issue is whether others believe them when they tell about such incidents. Do others, including the police, assume that because the victim has a disability such as a mobility impairment, the issue of consent is a murkier one than it is for non-disabled victims?

Victim History

Another problem reported by some police respondents arises when the victim has a history of making similar but unsubstantiated complaints. Although the police are trained to set their personal biases to one side, some police may simply be sceptical about the victim's latest story. Some respondents reported that the police, perhaps inadvertently, may not investigate such cases with the same thoroughness as they would other cases.

In the words of one police respondent, defence attorneys can be very skilled in dredging up this kind of information about the victim's past. Even if the police investigation is thorough and evidence to support the victim's complaint has been assembled, the victim's history could be used by the defence to discredit the victim's testimony. In such a case officers have to make a judgement call about the probability of the case standing up in court and about the wisdom of laying charges against the alleged perpetrator.

Some police respondents indicated that subsequent investigations can be affected when an individual who has been victimized returns to the same conditions in which she is likely to be victimized again. Despite training to set personal biases to one side, an officer may be less enthusiastic about investigating the subsequent victimization than if the victim were to have tried to avoid those dangerous circumstances. However, because of the lack of alternative supports, the victim may not think she has any choice *but* to return to the situation where she is likely to encounter the perpetrator again.

A victim's previous sexual activity could also "muddy the waters" of the investigation and trial proceeding. If the victim had consensual sex with the perpetrator in the past, it could be more difficult for the police to show that, during the incident in question, the victim withheld consent.

Victim Credibility

Many issues explored in this section of the report concern whether the police feel that victims and their testimony are likely to be viewed as credible in court. One police respondent pointed out that defence attorneys can confuse even non-disabled victims. What is the likelihood that the individual with a cognitive disability or mental health problem will be able to withstand the court process if they have been seriously traumatized, when their powers of recall will be severely taxed and when their personal credibility will be under fire? Will their testimony be perceived as believable? Will they as an individual be perceived as credible? Will the jury be sympathetic and flexible in its response to the victim's attempt to tell how she was victimized? Is the Crown attorney likely to go the extra mile in prosecuting the case to ensure that the victim's limitations are not viewed as a major liability in the proceeding? Will the judge be flexible in terms of how the testimony can be given? Before pressing charges, then, police have to arrive at a judgement based on many considerations. Where the victim has a disability, the range and seriousness of the factors that must be taken into account can be formidable.

The challenge of establishing the victim's credibility in turn is driven by three basic requirements inherent in the criminal justice process. First, the victim's claim against an alleged perpetrator must be established beyond reasonable doubt. The bias of the criminal proceeding is tilted in favour of the accused and the accused may have the upper hand in ability to manage jury perceptions. However, one police respondent indicated that where the alleged victim is obviously vulnerable to victimization and has a limitation that clearly affects her ability to satisfy the full rigour of the law, some leniency should be granted and the balance should be tilted in the victim's favour.

Second, the victim's testimony must be provided in a manner that is acceptable to the court. This means adult victims with disabilities must appear in court. A further de facto requirement is that victims must communicate in a manner that is understandable and acceptable to the court. As discussed earlier, the use of Bliss symbols, interpreters and technological aids to communication is becoming more common in courts and therefore less likely to present serious problems during trials. Some police respondents pointed out that problems nonetheless remain in the area of communication. They said the courts should be more flexible in terms of how they allow victim testimony to be given. The trauma of facing the perpetrator can make the victim withdraw emotionally and be unable to provide testimony. It can leave the victim so rattled that they even further garble what may already be a difficult story to tell. The view was expressed that the legal process ought to make some allowance for the victim to provide testimony from behind a screen or on video. Moreover, if the victim's mode of communication is idiosyncratic or at a different level than what the court would expect of someone the victim's age, the court should be required to take that into account and make the necessary accommodation. This was not occurring, according to some police respondents. The view was expressed that, failing these flexibilities, it is difficult in some instances for victims to have their stories heard in courts of law. Accordingly, police encounter a disincentive to press charges against the alleged perpetrator in the first place.

A third requirement is that the victim be able to

indicate to the court that they know what the truth is and that they understand it is a serious matter to tell anything but the truth. This is an abstraction that may mean little if anything to some victims. They may not be able to satisfy the court on this point. This problem presents yet another hurdle that may deter the police from laying charges.

Potential for Revictimization by the Court Process

Another set of difficulties facing the police concern the impact in human terms a criminal trial process would have on the victim. How will the victim react to the defence attorney's repeated efforts to discredit their testimony? This is of particular concern when the victim is often already intimidated by authority figures or has limited communication skills, or has been significantly traumatized, or has a weak self-image? If a defence attorney can rattle even non-disabled victims, what is likely to happen, under cross-examination, to someone whose confidence has been eroded from years of disability-related prejudice? What will likely happen if that victim also has a limited ability to cope with complex and stressful social situations, such as a criminal trial? Will they completely withdraw emotionally and be unable to provide testimony in any event? Will the victim become even more traumatized than they are at present? Some police respondents reported concern about victims becoming so distraught during trial that they would be at risk of being institutionalized. Again, although there was no indication during this research that these concerns would affect the investigation of the incident, it was reported that such issues could lead officers not to press charges against the alleged perpetrator — unless the victim clearly indicates a willingness to go through the court process despite the potential human costs.

Perpetrator History

If the alleged perpetrator is known by the police to have a prior history of victimizing others, this evidence could be useful in building the criminal case. However, one respondent pointed to a problem that may be limiting police insight into the background of perpetrators. The respondent indicated that at one time officers felt free to include in incident reports their gut hunches about whether an alleged perpetrator was involved in foul play. This was done even if the police had been unable to garner enough evidence to support laying formal charges. The view was expressed that, under the new *Freedom of Information Act*, the police are increasingly careful about what they include in their incident reports. They may be less inclined now than in the past to document their intuitions. Therefore, in searching incident reports for information about an alleged perpetrator, investigating officers may not be able to obtain potentially helpful clues about the perpetrator's character traits or past activities that have appeared suspicious — unless formal charges had been laid against him in the past.

A number of factors, then, affect the investigation and the outcome of cases involving victims with disabilities. Logistical, emotional, communication and evidentiary issues have to be sorted out during the criminal investigation. Some of these issues can affect whether police officers are able to obtain sufficient evidence to build cases. Other issues affect police officers' judgement of the case's solidity in court.

The research found that police have concerns about a victim's difficulties recalling details and the sequence of events during an incident in which they were victimized — difficulties that may or may not result principally from the victim's disability. The police also have concerns about the victim's possible embellishment of the details of the incident. These are concerns about what may be the victim's inadvertent admixture of detail or confusion spanning various incidents in which they may (or may not) have been victimized. Moreover, the police have concerns about: a communication mediator's potential to contaminate the evidence the victim is providing; what really happened in light of perhaps the confusing circumstances and lifestyle of the victim; the lack or weakness of forensic and other evidence (which could otherwise lend strength to the victim's story); and the possible absence of incriminating evidence from other incidents involving the same perpetrator.

There are further concerns about whether the victim will be able to "stick to his story" at the court date; concerns about the defence attorney's imputed skill and strategy in undermining the victim's testimony; concerns about the imputed sensitivity and flexibility of the trial judge and jury, should the case proceed that far; concerns about whether the victim might be revictimized by the trial process; concerns about the feasibility of the

Crown attorney's ability to establish that the victim withheld consent during the incident; concerns about the Crown attorney's skill and willingness to show that the victim's disability is not a liability during the trial proceedings; the victim's personal history (not only in reference to the alleged perpetrator, but also more generally whether they had previous, unsubstantiated claims of being victimized).

Many of these police concerns can ultimately be reduced to a concern about the victim's credibility in court. The police have to make a judgement call: is the victim's claim to having been victimized likely to be cogently substantiated beyond a reasonable doubt in a manner that is acceptable to the court? Is the court likely to believe that the victim is grounded in an abstract commitment to the truth. In the final analysis, if it appears to the police that the victim would not be able to survive the court process and have their testimony and personal credibility withstand the full rigours of the criminal trial, the police (and Crown attorney) may be disinclined to press charges.

The police, then, have enormous discretion to determine what happens to cases involving victims with disabilities.[42] The scope of this discretion is in itself disturbing. There are multiple grounds for the police not to press charges in what may be an extremely serious criminal matter. That discretion is all the more disturbing given the lack of police awareness about disability issues and the numerous other factors that can affect the reporting and initial police response to complaints. It would appear that the victims most disadvantaged in the process are those who are most seriously disabled and who are at greater risk than others of being in situations where they are vulnerable to victimization. Several police respondents indicated that such victims are at risk of falling through the cracks of the criminal justice system. Perhaps perpetrators know all this. Perhaps this is another reason why people with disabilities are more likely than others to be victimized.

Chapter 7

Police Data

I t has been noted in this report that precise data on the victimization of people with disabilities is not available at this point from the police. There is a general sense on the part of the police that people with disabilities are subject to victimization but, for a variety of reasons, police departments are unable to provide data to substantiate this. The lack of information about incidents of violence perpetrated against people with disabilities reported to the police, and police activities with respect to these incidents, can be attributed to a number of factors: (1) the traditional focus of policing and police data gathering; (2) the information reporting requirements for crime data imposed on police departments by Statistics Canada; (3) information management procedures in police communication centres; (4) the actual organization of the individual incident report, the report that is prepared by officers on the particulars of each complaint to which they have responded; (5) the organization and linkages between various units within any given department; and (6) politics.

First, the traditional focus of police departments is investigating cases, making arrests, laying charges and so on. To help the police in this work, departments have traditionally organized statistical information on the volume of complaints, the nature of complaints, whether charges were laid and on the outcome of the investigation — whether sentencing occurred. Information on perpetrators has also been systematically organized. Not until the past decade have the police begun to focus in a major way on the victims of crime. This new focus was adopted in recognition of the importance victims can play in assisting the criminal investigation. Therefore, police information management procedures lag behind actual policing practice. If it is possible to identify how many arrests were made in a particular region for sexual assault, there is little in the way of statistical data that would assist police to understand who is being victimized, their circumstances and the related risk factors.

Second, Statistics Canada's Department of Justice Statistics requires that police departments systematically gather and report crime data. The data gathering format that Statistics Canada requires — the Unified Crime Report (UCR) format — reflects the traditional focus of policing. Data is kept on details such as the number of specific kinds of complaint that come to the attention of the police, the number of charges laid for specific kinds of complaints. Statistics Canada does not require the police to gather data on victims. Police departments do have some discretion in organizing their own data management systems. Yet information management is to a large extent driven by Statistics Canada. The UCR format is under review and will require departments to gather much more victim-related data (such as marital status, ethnicity). Yet even the new format does not require reference to whether victims have disabilities. Without that, the police are no more likely in the future than they are at present to have statistical information on violence and disability.

Third, information management procedures in police communication centres conceivably could, but actually do not, enable identification of complaints by whether they originate in disability-related care-providing settings. Police information systems presently store computer information on "hazardous addresses." Information is noted on addresses where the police have had some prior involvement and where, for instance, firearms are known to be present. When a new complaint originates from that address and where an officer needs to be dispatched, the history of that address is available to the complaint-taker and dispatcher. Information about the specific dangers associated with that address is in turn relayed to the patrol officer. The same technology could be used to systematically track whether a given address or telephone number happens to be for a group home, a supported independent living arrangement, a rooming house in which elderly persons with disabilities are known to reside, a residential care facility and so on. Currently, however, police departments do not seem to organize information this way.[43] Only if the police have some prior involvement with an address, and if a particular danger to the police or others has been identified at that address, would patrol officers be flagged. Therefore, there is no systematic way of looking at the incidence or nature of complaints originating in any given year specifically from care settings. Yet such an analysis would yield at least partial insight into the magnitude and nature of the problem of violent victimization affecting people with disabilities.

Fourth, the organization of the police incident report (also called the occurrence report) is questionable. The incident report is the police record of the particulars of a complaint and subsequent investigation. Other documents relevant to the case are attached to this report such as forensic reports and victim impact statements. Information on whether or not the victim happens to have a disability may or may not be included in the incident report. Whether this occurs depends on two factors: (1) whether the officer thinks the victim's disability is directly relevant to the incident or investigation; and (2) the officer's general understanding of how disability *may* be related to victimization in a particular incident.

Assuming that the officer does believe the victim's disability has particular relevance to the case, that information, along with the other details of the investigation, would be included in the body of the incident report. The body of the report is different than the rest of the report in that it contains the officer's narrative of the investigation. Other sections of the report allow the officer to include only specific data such as the perpetrator's age and marital status, the sex of the victim and the nature of the offence. Once information has been included in the body of the incident report, the police have no way of systematically retrieving the disability-referenced information, although they can systematically retrieve information from the rest of the report. For example, a department may want to determine the stalking pattern of a perpetrator by looking at whether women with disabilities living in a particular region of the city were more likely than others to have complained of sexual assault in the past two years. The only way to determine this would be to read through each and every incident report of sexual assault cases occurring in that region and time frame and to look for mention of disability in the body of the incident reports. This is clearly an inefficient and costly way to obtain information. It poses a major disincentive for the police to even consider undertaking such an analysis. And where investigating officers have not considered victims' disabilities particularly relevant to the cases in the first instance, disability-related information may not be included in the incident reports.

Fifth, the way police departments are organized, and the nature of the communication and working linkages between units in any given department, affects the degree to which officers are knowledgeable about the violent victimization of people with disabilities. Commonly, police departments have a number of internal units with special functions or investigation areas. Many departments have a communications centre — an initial point of contact between complainants and the police — and a command centre for dispatching officers. It is also common for departments to have special units on child sexual assault, on major crime such as robbery, adult sexual assault, physical assault or elder abuse, and perhaps a unit on victim assistance or victim services which provides or arranges counselling and other support services for victims. A large department may have a unit of social workers who would liaise with community agencies that are involved in criminal investigations. A department may have a particular unit and command structure for beat or patrol officers. This structural complexity creates the potential for problems in the flow of information.

For example, those working in the major crime unit may have only informal or tenuous working contact with officers in the child sexual assault unit. If the officers working in child sexual assault are fielding disproportionate numbers of cases involving children with disabilities, officers in the major crime unit may not know about this. Depending on the police department, those working in victim assistance may only intervene in cases where the child sexual assault unit has exhausted its ability to provide the support which the child victim or family members require. Here, the victim assistance unit may have only fragmentary involvement with and insight into the caseload of the child sexual assault unit. Police social workers may have a good grasp of problems around abuse and assault in community service settings but tend to communicate specific knowledge about these issues on an as-needed basis to particular investigators in a given unit. Accordingly, those in victim assistance may not know what the social workers know. In some departments the patrol officer makes the initial response to a complaint but a criminal investigation unit does the detail work involved in the case. The beat officer may know little about the broader trends around victimization and disability, whereas senior investigators would likely be more aware of such trends. Those working in the communication centre will have initial information about complaints but may not be aware that a particular complaint of child sexual assault actually involved a number of victims with disabilities — something the child sexual assault team would know. In this way, bits and pieces of information on victimization and disability are communicated — and dispersed — through a complex system, with particular units tending to have insight only into their particular piece of the disability and violence problem.

This complex network of who knows what information is compounded because the organization of police departments varies significantly from municipality to municipality and region to region. In short, it is difficult to make generalizations about what the police know because the answer to that question will depend on who one talks to, the unit to which the officer is attached, their mandate, the kinds of contact (if any) they have with victims who have disabilities, their working links with other officers and the type of access they have to internal information.

Finally, community politics play an important role in specifying what the police should and should not be concerned about. For example, as the special interest groups concerned about child abuse took shape, police departments had to become better informed about this problem. As community groups raised the profile of wife assault, the police became better informed. As tensions began to rise between some visible minorities and the police, the police fell under pressure *not* to categorize people according to ethnicity. As youth gangs become more prevalent, police attention is turned from other issues. In the words of one respondent, "The policing community is driven by crisis."

This research found that victimization and disability has not yet achieved the profile of a "hot" political issue as far as the police are concerned. Until it does, the police are unlikely to feel that there is a community demand to become better informed in this area.

Chapter 8

Directions for Training and Policy Development

This research has pointed to a number of issues that confront the policing community in terms of the violent victimization of people with disabilities. This chapter looks at some of the implications of these issues for police training and policy development.

Training

There was a general sense among police respondents that the police receive little formal training on disability-related issues. What officers know is generally picked up through their work experience and through their general awareness and education about such matters. Where officers have received training, it has been in-service and has been delivered because their department has an interest in this area. In some instances, a community group or agency spurred police interest and may actually have provided the training.

It was generally, although not universally, agreed by police respondents that more officer training would be helpful. Views were somewhat mixed, however, on what officers need to know. Some respondents indicated that it would be useful to have general awareness-raising information. Issues that could be covered would include:

- the deinstitutionalization process and how this might affect community policing;

- myths and stereotypes about disability;

- patterns in the victimization of people with disabilities;

- risk factors particular to disability, and;

- general demographic information.

Other respondents indicated that the training needs to be practical. Themes to be covered could include:

- the implications of particular disabilities for victimization patterns and policing practice;

- practical aids to investigation concerning people with various limitations and, in particular, limited communication skills;

- how officers can work effectively in a multi-disciplinary way with other agencies;

- information on other agencies or community experts who may be able to assist the police and how they can help.

Here, individuals with disabilities and consumer/representative organizations could again play an important role in informing officers.

Police respondents had mixed views on the most

effective way to deliver the training. On the one hand, the value of formal instruction in police colleges was recognized. This fosters officer interaction and the sharing of experiences and policing tips, and provides a structure for training, without which the training might not occur. On other hand, it was widely recognized that officers have limited time in any given year to devote to formal training and that the dollars for this form of training are becoming scarcer. The value of brief and intense in-service training was noted. Involvement of people with disabilities as presenters may prove an effective way of putting information across, much in the same way as representatives of rape crisis centres are involved in some victim sensitivity training now received by police officers.

The approach to training should utilize a variety of instructional or information dissemination methods. These could include:

- informal learning resources, such as fact sheets and videos (these were seen as a potentially useful way of providing basic information and officers may be able to arrange brief time away from regular duties to review these);

- case studies that either did or did not end in the conviction of the perpetrator (which could be analyzed in workshops for the strengths and weaknesses of policing practice in those cases);

- role play — perhaps involving individuals with disabilities (for providing basic information, teaching competencies and establishing better contact between the police and the disability community);

- computer-based training (specifically on disability issues to supplement more traditional approaches to training).

In that the police are reliant on other agencies to know about victimization and even to assist during the investigation of cases, it would make sense for the training to target community groups and agencies. Themes to be covered could include:

- basic information on the signs of victimization and what social service staff can and *should* do about it;

- factors in the context of service delivery that can put people with disabilities at risk (so providers can "victim-proof" their services and procedures);

- model protocols or other mechanisms that have fostered effective collaboration between community agencies and the police in the prevention of and response to victimization;

- community policing and its implications and opportunities for community groups.

If the police cannot actually participate in the training that targets community agencies, departments could at least co-sponsor such events.

Policy Development

Some respondents indicated that what may be needed instead of a multiplicity of guidelines is a basic, "total person" approach to policing. This would be one general protocol that would apply regardless of who the victim might happen to be, but with specific pointers for police to ensure that the victim's particular needs are taken into account. Without guidelines, too much is left to the personal knowledge and sensitivity of individual officers and to the inclination of their department to actively detect victimization. At the very least it would be appropriate for generic protocols relating to wife assault, child abuse, child sexual abuse, adult sexual assault/abuse and senior abuse to clearly indicate that particular arrangements or considerations may be required and that specific agencies may need to be contacted to enable victims with disabilities to make their plight known to the police.

Regardless of what form the police protocol takes on victimization and disability, police should identify community agencies and community experts who can assist in investigations. This means having some form of current registry of information on such individuals and organizations, as well as clear communication and working links with these people and agencies. Model registries and information management systems for this kind of data should be more broadly disseminated within the policing community.

The police should also anticipate *not* being able to arrange support to assist victims or themselves during cases where the victims have disabilities. Contingency plans to secure the needed assistance from another source should be developed.

The police should assume that victimization of people with disabilities is a reality. Efforts should be made to ensure that police premises are physically accessible and that the complaint-making process is accessible to people with cognitive and sensory disabilities. At the very least, all police departments should have a Telephone Device for the Deaf (TDD).

Furthermore, the police should make it standard practice to become informed about individuals in neighbourhoods who are housebound because of their disabilities. In community policing, officers should inform themselves about various service environments where people may be at risk such as group homes, psychiatric institutions, multi-service institutions for persons with mental handicaps, lodging and rooming houses where people with disabilities are known to reside. The police should take the first step towards addressing this problem by establishing lines of communication with the people — "residents" and staff — in these settings. Good communication links, regular contact, a spirit of collaboration and partnership, and a healthy dose of candour between the police and representatives of these systems and agencies is essential for curbing and dealing with victimization once it occurs. The police may find that provincial and local social service departments, as well as local service-providing agencies and district planning councils, have useful information about these settings.

It is crucial for investigating officers to bear in mind that the individual who has been victimized is a complete human being with the full range of human emotions and needs — regardless of the nature or severity of their disability. Every effort must be made by the police to avoid stereotyping victims and to avoid assuming that having a disability means being less a person than others. Moreover, every effort should be made to elicit the victim's story. This will mean adopting a creative, flexible, persistent and, in some instances, patient approach to investigations. Perhaps the pace of questioning should be slowed down to give the individual time to think. If the questions are based on the assumption that the victim is anything other than a full human being with a full range of human feelings and experiences, the victim may feel demeaned and disinclined to respond. Victim responses that do not seem relevant to the question at hand should not be dismissed lightly as these responses may be the only way the victim can provide clues about the incident.

Police departments should make an effort to code incidents involving victims with disabilities in ways that allow systematic tracking of details such as frequencies, nature of incidents and victimization patterns. Although this information may not be immediately relevant to investigators, it is crucial for intelligent strategic planning by departments. Both the police and disability organizations should raise the profile of this issue with Statistics Canada's Department of Justice Statistics.

It is true that the police must, to a large extent, operate within the framework of the rules of evidence; however, these rules exclude many victims with disabilities from access to justice. Legal reform is needed to ensure that the criminal justice system guarantees justice for all, regardless of victims' communication needs and intellectual abilities. Yet the police could play an important role in systemic reform. The police are currently playing the role of the "gatekeepers" to justice. In exercising the discretion to screen cases from coming to the attention of the courts, the police are also in a position to prevent the court and legal system from perceiving the need for systemic reform. This seems to be exactly what is occurring. Instead, the police should open the gates to justice and bring to the attention of the courts all cases in which victimization is known or suspected. This may mean bringing less "solid" cases to court. If this does not happen it is difficult to imagine how attorneys, judges and politicians are to become aware of the serious flaws in the present justice system that effectively deny justice to those who are most vulnerable to victimization.

Other Considerations

All social services should be required to have reporting protocols. Guidelines should ensure that criminal or potentially criminal matters are brought to police attention. There should be strict requirements for staff to report incidents where victimization is suspected. There should be monitoring and enforcement of these reporting requirements — and probably "whistle-blower" protection for those who do report victimization. The police may be able to play a constructive role in working out the details of these protocols with local service providers. Government funding for service-providing agencies should be contingent on such reporting procedures being in place.

It is recognized that the police do not have absolute control over their own budgets. However, there should be a clear government and police commitment to fund victim assistance programs. Funding levels ought to respect the need for victim assistance personnel to become well informed on a range of issues relating to disability, victimization and policing. In addition, it is crucial that the rules of evidence and other matters pertaining to the court system be examined with a view to ensuring that all people who are victimized, regardless of disability, have access to justice.

The violent victimization of people with disabilities is a criminal matter, not just another social service issue or political fad. It is a serious problem — a vicious scandal — that has been driven underground and covered up for too long. If people with disabilities are more at risk of victimization than others, this point has largely escaped the attention of the policing community. If victims with disabilities are less likely than others to have access to justice, this point seems to be taken in stride by the criminal justice system more broadly. Yet perpetrators seem to know only too well that a very large segment of the population is at risk. The question remains: when, if not now, is the time to act?

Notes

1. *Toronto Star,* April 27, 1993.

2. *Toronto Star,* January 15, 1993.

3. *Toronto Star,* August 17, 1992.

4. *The Gazette,* Montreal, July 22, 1992.

5. *Toronto Star,* April 25, 1992.

6. *Toronto Star,* March 25, 1992.

7. *Journal of Family Violence,* Vol. 3. No. 1, 1988.

8. Statistics Canada has conducted a major survey on violence against women in Canada and will be releasing reports shortly. In principle, Statistics Canada will be able to examine issues concerning the victimization of women with disabilities on the basis of that survey (Violence Against Women Survey).

9. These terms are used widely within the policing community. However, it is recognized that police officers may define the terms more broadly to include any criminal action regardless of violence (e.g., theft) and the people who are directly affected by those actions.

10. Bayley (1991) points out that, while the mission statements of most police departments express a

commitment to community policing, substantive commitment by the police to this philosophy has not always been realized. Yet, he observes that if there has been much police posturing about community policing, there has also been a considerable amount of genuine program innovation.

11. Bayley (1991), however, has suggested that the problem of work "overload" may be less an actuality than a matter of police perception.

12. About the only detailed disability-related information a department is likely to have about people who are perhaps at risk of victimization would be contained in the department's Wandering Persons registry. This is a printed (i.e., not computer-based) directory of information that some departments are using on local citizens who have Alzheimer's disease.

13. Not all respondents were concerned about this lack of police data.

14. This perception may be a function of the specific roles and types of caseloads of those who were interviewed.

15. Although perhaps not violent per se, incidents like fraud and theft were identified by police respondents as crimes perpetrated against older persons with disabilities. Consumer respondents saw theft by care-givers as being a problem that affects people with disabilities quite broadly, regardless of age. This view is confirmed in other research studies (Ulicny, 1990). Given that many people with disabilities are poor, the theft of money is likely to

be of small amounts. If such a theft is brought to the attention of the police at all, it is likely to be viewed as a minor offence. It may even go unreported because of the victim's perception that the police are likely to dismiss the matter. Yet it is worth noting that a small amount of money taken from a poor person can, in relative terms, be a serious matter. Whether the police make contextual judgements about the relative seriousness of such offences is not clear.

16. Statistics Canada, Health and Activity Limitation Survey (1986), micro-data set.

17. There are no grounds for assuming, however, that this particular department would or should have been better informed than other police departments about TDD usage patterns and about what to expect in terms of the frequency of TDD-user complaints.

18. The discrepant views on age could be related to the particular mandate of the individuals who were interviewed for this research and the segment of the population with which they have the most contact.

19. Various research reports cited in this study, however, do suggest that people with disabilities are more likely than others to be victimized.

20. If the police have any information at all on disability in their particular geographic region, it would likely be general demographic information obtained from organizations like Social Planning Councils.

21. Stimpson and Best, 1991; Rinear, 1985.

22. See also Bajt and Pope (1989) for results of research on psychologists who admitted to having sexual relations with their child clients. Bajt, T. R., and Pope, K.S. (1989). "Therapist-Patient Sexual Intimacy Involving Children and Adolescents" [Special issue: Children and their development: Knowledge base, research agenda, and social policy application], *American Psychologist,* 44(2), p. 455.

23. These figures are from Statistics Canada's 1986 Health and Activity Limitations Survey (HALS) microdata set for adults in households. The figures do not include persons in institutional or other residential care settings, where there is greater reliance on caregivers for support in the area of personal care and where care-givers would generally have more control over persons with disabilities.

24. A variable was derived from HALS 1986 (Adults in Households) to identify people who require more assistance than what they were then receiving in a variety of daily living activities.

25. Statistics Canada, *Children and Youth with Disabilities in Canada,* The 1986 Health and Activity Limitation Survey, Ottawa, 1992.

26. HALS, 1986.

27. One of the respondents indicated that their department has three sign language interpreters on staff in their communication centre. Another indicated that several officers are being trained in these skills.

28. How widely this is the case is beyond the scope of the present research.

29. How widely protocols are in place in the social service sector to ensure reporting of the victimization of people with disabilities is not clear and is beyond the scope of the present research to determine.

30. These include potential for litigation based on claims of negligence or collusion.

31. It was found that police training and normal procedure are designed to require officers to hear victim complaints without prejudging the situation. As one officer pointed out, "Sometimes the less believable the complaint sounds, the more believable it actually is."

32. Some respondents indicated that the police would cover the costs of involving family or other informal supports where travel, meals or accommodation expenses are involved.

33. These needs might be addressed through informal supports as well, such as family or friends.

34. Police respondents generally indicated that the only means their departments have for making such an assessment are informal letters of thanks or complaint.

35. That is, the victim may construe the investigating officer to be an authority figure.

36. However, the police may not always be able to find someone who is able to perform the role of communicator.

37. For example, a police respondent reported on one case in which a police investigator and a Crown attorney had visited a victim over the course of several months to ensure that the person was able to recall the particulars of the story she had initially told the investigators.

38. Strictly speaking, corroboration is not required for cases involving sexual assault/abuse. However, in these as in other cases, the greater the amount and the better the quality of the evidence that the police can obtain, the stronger the case the police can build. In the words of one respondent, "It never hurts to have corroborating evidence."

39. Medical doctors and hospital workers are provided with specific "kits" for obtaining this kind of evidence from victims.

40. If the complaint is about child sex assault or abuse involving a perpetrator who is not an immediate family member (e.g., not the victim's father or brother), and if the alleged perpetrator has children of his own, the investigation may focus on those children on the assumption that the perpetrator may be abusing them as well. Evidence to that effect would lend support to the victim's story.

41. Others involved in the investigation could include child welfare workers (e.g., Children's Aid Society social workers), educators, hospital staff, workers from women's hostels, and supported work staff.

42. It is important to point out that the police consult with Crown attorneys during investigations and the decisions reached by the police are influenced by the Crown attorney's input.

43. A respondent at one department, however, did indicate that such an arrangement has been implemented for group homes in the department's catchment area.

Bibliography

Alicia-Diaz, A. (1990). "Child Sexual Abuse: Investigative problems." *The Police Chief,* Vol. 57, Oct., p. 111.

Anderson, D. T. and Hanson, R. (1990). "City Police Provide Services at a State Mental Hospital." *The Police Chief,* Vol. 57, Oct., p. 92.

Arcaya, J.M. (1989). "The Police and the Emotionally Disturbed: A psychoanalytic theory of intervention." *International Journal of Offender Therapy and Criminology,* 33(1), pp. 37-48.

"Arrest Policy for Domestic Calls Takes Away Officer Discretion." *The Police Chief,* Vol. 54, Sept. 1987, pp. 20-21.

Baca, S. (1987). "Domestic Violence: One police department's solution." *The Police Chief,* Vol. 54, Aug., pp. 40-41.

Bajt, T.R. and Pope, K.S. (1989). "Therapist-Patient Sexual Intimacy Involving Children and Adolescents." [Special Issue: Children and their development: Knowledge base, resource agenda, and social policy application]. *American Psychologist,* 44(2), p. 455.

Bayley, David H. (1991). *Managing the Future: Prospective issues in Canadian policing, 1991-92.* Ottawa: Ministry of the Solicitor General of Canada, pp. 107-108.

Bean, P. et al. (1991). *Out of Harm's Way: MIND's research into police and psychiatric action under Section 136 of the Mental Health Act.* London, UK: MIND Publications.

Beane, M. and Jackson, E. (1985). "Family Trauma Team." *The Police Chief,* Vol. 52, Jan., pp. 31-33.

Berk, R., Berk, S.F. and Newton, O. (1984). "Cops On Call: Summoning the police to the scene of spousal violence." *Law and Society Review,* 18(3), pp. 479-498.

Berkman, A. (1984-86). "Professional Responsibility Confronting Sexual Abuse of People with Disabilities." *Sexuality and Disability,* 7(3/4), Fall/Winter, pp. 89-95.

Besharov, D.J. (1986). "Child Abuse: Arrest and prosecution decision-making." *American Criminal Law Review,* 24(2), pp. 315-377.

Billinghurst, J. and Hackler, J. (1982). "In My Opinion: The mentally retarded in prison: Is justice denied?" *Canadian Journal of Criminology,* 24(3), p. 341.

Blake, R. (1987). "Boarding Home Residents: New underclass in the mental health system." *Health and Social Work,* Vol. 12, Spring, pp. 85-90.

Blatt, B. (1980). "The Pariah Industry: A diary from purgatory and other places." In Gerbner, G., Ross, C.J. and Zigler, E. (eds.). *Child Abuse: An agenda for action.* New York: Oxford University Press.

Boyd, E. (1985). *Crisis Intervention and Conflict Management Training in the R.C.M.P.* Ottawa: Ministry of the Solicitor General of Canada.

Brecci, M. and Simons, R. (1987). "An Examination of Organizational and Individual Factors that Influence Police Response to Domestic Disturbances." *Journal of Police Science and Administration,* Vol. 15, June, pp. 93-104.

Browne, S., Connors, D. and Stern, N. (1985). *With the Power of Each Breath: A disabled women's anthology.* Pittsburgh: Cleis Press.

Buchanan, D. and Chasnoff, P. (1986). "Family Crisis Intervention Program: What works and what doesn't." *Journal of Police Science and Administration,* Vol. 14, June, pp. 161-168.

Burden, O.P. (1991). "Crime Prevention for the Disabled: What police agencies can and should do." *Crime Control Digest,* 25(38), Sept.

Burstow, Bonnie and Weitz, Don (eds.). (1988). *Shrink Resistant: The struggle against psychiatry in Canada.* Vancouver: New Star Books.

Canadian Institute of Child Health (CICH). (1989). *The Health of Canada's Children: A CICH profile.* Ottawa.

Canadian Women's Studies. (1991). *Violence Against Women: Strategies for change.* 12(1), Fall.

Cash, T. and Valentine, D. (1987). "A Decade of Adult Protective Services: Case characteristics." *Journal of Gerontological Social Work,* 10(3/4), pp. 47-60.

Cole, S.S. (1984-86). "Facing the Challenges of Sexual Abuse in Persons with Disabilities." *Sexuality and Disability,* 7(3/4), Fall/Winter, pp. 71-88.

Conley, R.W., Luckasson, R. and Bouthilet, G. N. (1992). *The Criminal Justice System and Mental Retardation: Defendants and victims.* Baltimore: Paul H. Brookes Publishing Co.

Conners, G. (1990). "Domestic Disputes: A model pro-arrest policy." *Law and Order,* 38(2), pp. 66-67.

Conrad, M. and Jahn, T. (1985). "The Family Stress Team Approach In Curbing Domestic Violence." *The Police Chief,* Vol. 52, June, pp. 66-67.

Crews, W. and Cochran, S. (1989) "Memphis Police Department's Crisis Intervention Team." *Law and Order,* 37(8), pp. 66-70.

Davis, R. (1987). "The Domestic Violence Prevention Project: A proactive response to familial abuse." *The Police Chief,* Vol. 54, Aug., pp. 42-44.

Dent, H.R. (1986). "An Experimental Study of the Effectiveness of Different Techniques of Questioning a Mentally Handicapped Child Witness." *British Journal of Clinical Psychology,* 25(1), pp. 13-17.

Derksen, M. and Van Rossum, G.J. (1987). "Police Clients with Mental Problems: A study in cooperation between the police and mental health care services in Rotterdam." *Maandblad Geestelijke Volks-gezondheid,* 42(1), pp. 35-49.

Docherty, J. (1989). *Investigating Child Abuse in Residential Care Settings.* Toronto: James Docherty & Associates.

Dolon, R., Hendricks, J. and Meagher, S. (1986). "Police Practices and Attitudes Towards Domestic Violence." *Journal of Police Science and Administration,* Vol. 14, Sept., pp. 187-192.

Federal Bureau of Investigation and Metro Dade Police Department. (1983). *Proceedings: Forensic Science Symposium on the Analysis of Sexual Assault Evidence.* Quantico, VA: Forensic Science Research and Training Center, Laboratory Division, FBI Academy.

Fein, E. and Knaut, S.A. (1986). "Crisis Intervention and Support Working with Police." *Social Casework,* 67(5), pp. 276-282.

Finn, P. and Sullivan, M. (1989). "Police Handling the Mentally Ill: Sharing responsibility with the mental health system." *Journal of Criminal Justice,* 17(1), pp. 1-14.

Fulmer, T. (1988). "Elder Abuse." In Straus, M. (ed.). *Abuse and Victimization Across the Life Span.* Baltimore: John Hopkins.

Gaudreault, A. (1991). "The Police and Crime Victims: A still fragile partnership." *Canadian Journal of Criminology,* 33(3/4), pp. 459-468.

Gerbner, G., Ross, C.J., and Zigler, E. (eds.). (1990). *Child Abuse: An agenda for action.* New York: Oxford University Press.

Gilmartin, K.M. (1986). "The Effects of Psychiatric Deinstitutionalization on Community Policing." *The Police Chief,* Vol. 53, Dec., pp. 37-39.

Gnaedinger, N. (1989). *Working Together: National Forum on Family Violence, June 18-21, 1989, Discussion paper: Elder abuse.* Ottawa: Family Violence Prevention Division, Health and Welfare Canada.

Goldstein, A., Monti, P., Sardino, T. and Green, D. (1977). *Police Crisis Intervention.* Kalamazoo, Michigan: Behaviordelia.

Groce N. (1988) "Special Groups at Risk of Abuse: The disabled." In Straus, M. (ed.). *Abuse and Victimization Across the Life Span.* Baltimore: John Hopkins.

"Group Home Abuse File." Newspaper Clippings. North York: The Roeher Institute Information Services.

Hanmer, J. and Maynard, M. (1987). *Women, Violence and Social Control.* Atlantic Highlands, NJ: Humanities Press International Inc.

Health and Welfare Canada. (1991). *Family Violence, Situation Paper and Backgrounders.* Family Violence Prevention Division.

Health and Welfare Canada. (1984). *The Badgely Committee Report.* Ottawa.

Health and Welfare Canada. (1991). *Reaching for Solutions: Report of the special advisor on child sexual abuse.* Ottawa: National Clearinghouse on Family Violence.

Hertl, M. (1988). "The 'Helpless Person:' Tomorrow it may be you. Appeal for a more medical approach." *Deutsche Polizie,* 37(4), pp. 17-20.

Hoefkens, A. and Allen, D. (1990). "Evaluation of a Specialized Behaviour Unit for People with Mental Handicaps and Challenging Behaviour." *Journal of Mental Deficiency Research,* Vol. 34, June, pp. 213-228.

Holbrook, T. (1989). "Policing Sexuality in a Modern State Hospital." *Hospital and Community Psychiatry,* 40(1), pp. 75-79.

Kalinich, D. and Senese, J.D. (1987). "Police Discretion and the Mentally Disordered in Chicago: A reconsideration." *Police Studies,* 10(4), pp. 185-191.

Keith, L. (1992). "Who Cares Wins? Women, caring and disability." *Disability, Handicap and Society,* 7(2), pp. 167-175.

Kohan, M., Pothier, P. and Norbeck, J. (1987). "Hospitalized Children with History of Sexual Abuse: Incidence and care issues." *American Journal of Orthopsychiatry,* 57(2), April, pp. 258-264.

Krents, E., Schulman, V. and Brenner, S. (1987). "Child Abuse and the Disabled Child: Perspectives for parents." *Volta-Review,* 89(5), Sept., pp. 78-95.

LeGrand, C. (1984). "Mental Hospital Regulation and the Safe Environment." *Law, Medicine and Health Care,* 12(6), pp. 236-242.

Lloyd-Bostock, S. and Shapland, J. (1986). "The Police and Criminal Evidence Act 1984: Some continuing questions for psychologists." *Bulletin of the British Psychological Society,* Vol. 39, pp. 241-245.

Maher, R. and George, V. (1986). "An Innovative Approach to Service: Hartford's community response division." *The Police Chief,* Vol. 53, Dec., p. 26.

Maibaum, M. (1985). "Staff Defensiveness and Legal Advocacy in a California State Hospital." *American Journal of Forensic Psychology,* 3(1), pp. 29-37.

Martell, D. (1991). "Homeless Mentally Disordered Offenders and Violent Crimes: Preliminary research findings." *Law and Human Behaviour,* 15(4), pp. 333-347.

Mason, M.A. (1991). "The McMartin Case Revisited: The conflict between social work and criminal justice." *Social Work,* 36(5), pp. 391-395.

Masuda, S. (1988). "$22 M for Transition Houses - But Can We Use Them?" *Thriving,* Newsletter of DAWN Canada, 1(1).

Masuda, S. and Riddington, J. (1990). *Meeting our Needs: Access Manual for Transition Houses.* Vancouver: DAWN (DisAbled Women's Network) Canada.

Mawby, R. and Gill, M. (1988). "Picking up the Pieces." *Police Review,* 96(4944), pp. 130-131.

McAfee, J. K. and Gural, M. (1988). "Individuals with Mental Retardation and the Criminal Justice System: The view from the State's Attorneys General." *Mental Retardation,* 26(1), pp. 5-12.

McClenahan, C. (1990). "Victim Services: A positive police community effort." *The Police Chief,* Vol. 57, Oct., p. 104.

McKenzie, J. (1990). "Dealing with the Mentally Disordered." *Police Review,* 98(5049), pp. 284-285.

McNiel, D.E. (1991). "Characteristics of Persons Referred by the Police to Psychiatric Emergency Room." *Hospital and Community Psychiatry,* 42(4), pp. 425-427.

McPherson, C. (1990). *Responding to the Abuse of People With Disabilities.* Toronto: Advocacy Research Centre for the Handicapped.

Mederer, H.J. and Gelles, R.J. (1989). "Compassion or Control: Intervention in cases of wife abuse." *Journal of Interpersonal Violence,* 4(1), pp. 25-43.

Menzies, R.J. (1987). "Psychiatrists in Blue: Police apprehension of mental disorder and dangerousness." *Criminology,* 25(3), pp. 429-453.

Melberg, K. (1984). "The Silent Epidemic." *SAMR Dialect,* Aug., p. 10.

Mulick, J.A. (1990). "The Ideology and Science of Punishment in Mental Retardation." *American Journal of Mental Retardation,* 95(2), Sept., pp. 142-173.

Mullen, C. (1988). "Center Agrees Disabled People Face Higher Risk of Sexual Attack." *Edmonton Journal,* Sept. 15, p. B5.

Musick, J.L. (1984). "Patterns of Institutional Sexual Assault." *Response to Violence in the Family and Sexual Assault,* 7(3), pp. 1-2, 10-11.

Newbern, V. B. (1989). "Sexual Victimization of Child and Adolescent Patients." *Image: The Journal of Nursing Scholarship,* 21(1), pp. 10-13.

Nibert, D., Cooper, S. and Crossmaker, M. (1989). "Assaults Against Residents of a Psychiatric Institution: Residents' history of abuse." *Journal of Interpersonal Violence,* 4(3), Sept., p. 342

Ombudsman of British Columbia. (1987). *The Use of Criminal Record Checks to Screen Individuals Working with Vulnerable People.* Public Report No. 5. Victoria: Queen's Printer for British Columbia.

Parker, W. (1985). "Domestic Violence and Potential Liability for Police." *The Police Chief,* Vol. 52, Dec., p. 16.

Pillemer, K. and Finklehor, D. (1989). "Causes of Elder Abuse: Caregiver stress vs. problem relatives." *American Journal of Orthopsychiatry,* Vol. 59, pp. 179-187.

Pogrebin, M.K. and Poole, E.D. (1987). "Deinstitutionalization and Increased Arrest Rates Among the Mentally Disordered." *Journal of Psychiatry and Law,* 15(1), pp. 117-127.

Quine, L. and Pahl, J. (1985). "Examining the Causes of Stress in Families with Mentally Handicapped Children." *British Journal of Social Work,* Vol. 15, pp. 501-517.

Rabb, J. and Rindfleisch, N.A. (1985). "A Study to Define and Assess Severity of Institutional Abuse/ Neglect." *Child Abuse and Neglect,* 9(2), pp. 285-294.

Riddington, J. (1989) *Beating the Odds: Violence and women with disabilities.* (Position paper 2). Vancouver: DAWN (DisAbled Women's Network) Canada.

Rindfleisch, N. and Bean, G.J. (1988). "Willingness to Report Abuse and Neglect in Residential Facilities." *Child Abuse and Neglect,* 12(4), pp. 509-520.

Rinear, E.E. (1985). "Sexual Assault and the Handicapped Victim." In Burgess, A.W. (ed.). *Rape and Sexual Assault.* New York: Garland Publishing, pp. 139-145.

The Roeher Institute. (1992). *No More Victims: Manuals to guide the police, social workers and counsellors, family and the legal community in addressing the sexual abuse of people with mental handicaps.* North York.

The Roeher Institute. (1988). *Vulnerable: Sexual abuse and people with a mental handicap.* North York.

Rosenbaum, D. (1987). "Coping with Victimization: The effects of police intervention on victims' psychological readjustment." *Crime and Delinquency,* Vol. 33, Oct., pp. 502-517.

Ruane, J.M. and Cerulo, K.A. (1990). "The Police and Community Mental Health Centres: The transition from penal to therapeutic control." *Law and Policy,* 12(2), pp. 137-154.

Sales, G.N. (1991). "A Comparison of Referrals by Police and Other Sources to a Psychiatric Emergency Service." *Hospital and Community Psychiatry,* 42(9), pp. 950-951.

Schilling, R.F. and Schinke, S.P. (1984). "Personal Coping and Social Support for Parents of Handicapped Children." *Children and Youth Services Review,* 6(3), pp. 195-206.

Schilling, R.F., Kirkham, M.A. and Schinke, S.P. (1986). "Do Child Protection Services Neglect Developmentally Disabled Children?" *Education and Training of the Mentally Retarded,* 21(1), March, pp. 21-26.

Schor, D.P. (1987). "Sex and Sexual Abuse of Developmentally Disabled Adolescents." *Seminars in Adolescent Medicine,* 3(1), pp. 1-7.

Skogun, W. and Wycoff, M. (1987). "Some Unexpected Effects of a Police Service for Victims." *Crime and Delinquency,* Vol. 33, Oct., pp. 490-501.

Sobsey, D. and Varnhagen, C. (1988). *Sexual Abuse, Assault and Exploitation of People with Disabilities.* Ottawa: Health and Welfare Canada.

Stainton, T. (1988). "Aversive Conditioning: Necessity or failure?" In The Roeher Institute. *The Language of Pain: Perspectives on behaviour management.* North York.

Statistics Canada. (1992). *Children and Youth with Disabilities in Canada: The 1986 Health and Activity Limitation Survey.* Ottawa.

Statistics Canada. (1986). *Health and Activity Limitation Survey Micro-Data Set.* Ottawa

Steinman, M. (1990). "Lowering Recidivism Among Men Who Batter Women." *Journal of Police Science and Administration,* 17(2), pp. 124-132.

Stimpson, L. and Best, M. (1991). *Courage Above All: Sexual assault against women with disabilities.* Toronto: DisAbled Women's Network (DAWN) Canada.

Sullivan, P.M. and Scanlon, J.M. (1987). "Therapeutic Issues." In Garbarino, J., Brookhouser, P. and Authier, K. (eds.). *Special Children - Special Risks: The maltreatment of children with disabilities.* New York: Aldine de Gruyter.

Sullivan, P.M., Vernon, M. and Scanlon, J.M. (1987). "Sexual Abuse of Deaf Youth." *American Annals of the Deaf,* 132(4), pp. 256-262.

Teplin, L. (1986). *Keeping the Peace: The parameters of police discretion in relation to the mentally disordered.* Washington, DC: U.S Department of Justice, National Institute of Justice.

Teplin, L. (1985). "The Criminality of Mental Illness: A dangerous misconception." *American Journal of Psychiatry,* 42(5), pp. 593-599.

Tilelli, J.A., Turek, D. and Jaffe, A.C. (1980). "Sexual Abuse of Children: Clinical findings and implications for management." *New England Journal of Medicine,* Vol. 302, pp. 319-323.

Ulicny, G., White, G., Bradford, B. and Mathews, M. (1990). "Consumer Exploitation by Attendants: How often does it happen and can anything be done about it?" *Rehabilitation Counselling Bulletin,* 33(3), March, pp. 240-246.

Underwood, N. (1989). "Sex and Scandal: An inquiry hears graphic allegations of abuse." *Maclean's,* Vol. 102, p. 84.

Walker, D. (1985). "Domestic Response Team," *RCMP Gazette,* 47(2), pp. 7-10.

Warner, R. (1989). "Deinstitutionalization: How did we get where we are?" *Journal of Social Issues,* 45(3), pp. 17-30.

Weller, M.P.I. and Weller, B.G.A. (1988). "Crime and Mental Illness." *Medicine, Science and Law,* 28(1), pp. 38-46.

Wickham-Searl, P. (1992). "Careers in Caring: Mothers of children with disabilities." *Disability, Handicap and Society,* 7(1), pp. 5-17.

Wirtz, P. and Harrell, A. (1987). "Police and Victims of Physical Assault." *Criminal Justice and Behaviour,* Vol. 14, March, pp. 81-92.

Worder, R. and Pollitz, A. (1984). "Police Arrests in Domestic Disturbances: A further look." *Law and Society Review,* 18(1), pp. 105-119.

Worthington, G.M. (1984). "Sexual Exploitation and Abuse of People with Disabilities." *Response to Victimization of Women and Children,* 7(2), pp. 7-8.

Wright, J.N. (1990). "Is Your Job Killing You? A study of assault on South Australian police officers." *National Police Response Unit Review,* Vol. 6, pp. 34-40.

Zantal-Weiner, K. (1987). *Child Abuse and the Handicapped Child.* Reston, VA: ERIC Clearinghouse on Handicapped and Gifted Children, Digest No. 446.

Selected Publications of The Roeher Institute

- **No More Victims:** Manuals to address the sexual abuse of people with a mental handicap, 1992-1993

- **Sexual Abuse Prevention Programs and Mental Handicap,** 1989

- **On Target?** Canada's Employment-Related Programs for Persons with Disabilities, 1993

- **Direct Dollars:** A Study of Individualized Funding in Canada, 1993

- **Vulnerable:** Sexual Abuse and People with an Intellectual Handicap, 1988

- **Poor Places:** Disability-Related Residential and Support Services, 1990

- **Nothing Personal:** The Need for Personal Supports in Canada, 1993

- **Income Insecurity:** The Disability Income System in Canada, 1988

- **Changing Canadian Schools:** Perspectives on Disability and Inclusion, 1991

- **Quality Child Care for All:** A Guide to Integration, 1992

- **Right off the Bat:** A Study of Inclusive Child Care in Canada, 1993

- **Literacy and Labels:** A Look at Literacy Policy and People with a Mental Handicap, 1990

- **The Power to Choose:** An Examination of Service Brokerage and Individualized Funding as Implemented by the Community Living Society, 1991

For more information please contact:

The Roeher Institute Kinsmen Building, York University, 4700 Keele Street, North York, Ontario M3J 1P3 Telephone: (416) 661-9611 Fax: (416) 661-5701 TDD: (416) 661-2023

entourage: **The Roeher Institute's quarterly bilingual magazine**

entourage is on the leading edge of constructive ideas and theories in the field of intellectual and other disabilities. Its timely articles identify the latest directions for change and new ways of understanding inclusive communities and economies.